UNCHAIN YOUR BRAIN

Move Beyond Fear and Discouragement,
and Start Living with Purpose

Mark Ashe

Published by Author Academy Elite
PO Box 43, Powell, OH 43065
www.AuthorAcademyElite.com

Identifiers:
LCCN: 2020922144
ISBN: 978-1-64746-604-6 (paperback)
ISBN: 978-1-64746-605-3 (hardback)
ISBN: 978-1-64746-606-0 (ebook)

Available in paperback, hardback, e-book

Cover design by Perry Yeldham, 21 Thirteen Design, Inc.
perry@21thirteen.com

Other Books by Mark Ashe

The Common Sense for a Prosperous Life series

Riches Beyond the Bling
Invest Like a Wealth Manager
The Entry-Level CEO
Private Choices, Public Power

*… [A]ll you need is to know what you want,
and to want it badly enough
so that it will stay in your thoughts.*

—Wallace D. Wattles

CONTENTS

AUTHOR'S NOTES

As I sit in my study, I am looking at a framed photograph of Orison Swett Marden. Mr. Marden wrote a lot in the late 1800s about character and its relationship to wealth. He was orphaned as a young boy and put out to hard labor as little more than a slave. Overworked and underfed, he was often beaten by a tyrannical master. Half-starving most of the time, he would sneak an extra bite of food when he found it, terrified of the beating he would receive if he were caught. With no one to aid him, encourage him, guide him—or even love him—he yet *lifted himself* to become one of the preeminent authors of his time. He wrote with authority on the subject of rising from limiting circumstances to achieve a satisfying place in life.

After submitting his first book, *Pushing to the Front,* to several publishers—unsure if any would be willing to print it—to his surprise, publishers actually fought each other over the rights to the book. That book was reprinted again and again and distributed around the globe! Governments bought the book for nationwide distribution in their schools.

In a later book, *Good Manners: A Passport to Success*, Mr. Marden penned twenty-seven words that set the course of my adult life:

It is the duty of every young person, and especially of every young man, to set about the task of becoming financially independent. The amount is inconsequential.

From the first time I read those words, now thirty-five years ago, those two sentences became my personal philosophy—and my obsession. They became my life's field manual and I began a passionate pursuit to attain financial independence.

Even though I still am not a financial sophisticate or a business tycoon (or even had those things as goals), by the age of forty-five I lived on a beautiful farm in the foothills of the North Georgia mountains and I was debt-free and financially independent. My wife and children were living a blessed life, and I was there with them to enjoy every day of it.

Armies issue their new soldiers a "field manual." When faced with a decision, a soldier can go to the manual, refer to the appropriate section, and see quickly what to avoid and what course of action to take to increase the odds of a desirable outcome. I have long been of the opinion that, if a practical reference manual could be written for making the major decisions of life—especially if written in an engaging style—a great need would be met for us civilians fighting the battles of life.

To that end, I have written the Common Sense for a Prosperous Life book series, five quick-read handbooks that cut straight to the heart of the most important issues of life:

1. earning and spending,
2. saving and investing,
3. running a business,
4. creative thinking, intention, and focus, and
5. mature judgment, marriage, and other personal choices.

But I chose to write these books—including the one you now hold in your hand—with great reluctance. Here's how it happened.

In 2008 I witnessed the global financial meltdown that would shake the worlds markets for years, but I had seen it coming. Almost all of the "prosperity" everyone seemed to be enjoying leading up to the crash was an illusion built on excessive debt and other bad decisions.

During those earlier years of society-wide excessive borrowing and spending, an unbidden idea kept pushing itself up, forcing its way into my mind. The thought seemed preposterous—an errant notion passing through the wrong mind—and, at first, I treated it exactly like that. Over time, however, it grew into a conviction that I could not escape, even as I continued to thrust it away.

Here is that thought:

Mark, *you* write a book that will give the reader a healthy foundation for decisions concerning money, business, and personal life. This current foolishness—the "You can get rich quick and live rich now; here's how!" mantra being fed to the unsophisticated and gullible public by new money magazines, how-I-got-rich authors, and breathless news anchors on financial channels excitedly reporting the day's Wall Street winners—must be confronted.

The healthy intention to become an independent, balanced, self-restrained adult has been lost. Independence, not consumption, must once again be held up for all to see as the proper purpose of labor. *You* are to write a book that will spell out—in simple terms—a practical mindset business, and life that will provide a road map to help ordinary men and women see make wiser choices.

As I have said, I repeatedly dismissed this most unwelcome impulse. After many years of hard work in my own business, I had no appetite for such a time-consuming task, nor did I feel competent. Not only did I feel unqualified to write about these things—after all, my accomplishments are modest when compared to those of the wealthy best-selling authors so prevalent on bookshelves—but I did not believe I had any gift at all for writing, on *any* subject. I did not want, nor have I ever desired, to write a book.

For several years, I continued to consider the thought ridiculous, but then I had a health scare that turned out to be a false alarm. That was the turning point for me. Why? Because the first thought that went through my mind when I feared bad news was not for my family or myself. To my shock, it was instead, "I should have written that book."

That's when I realized this work was something I *must* do, I was *intended* to do, whether or not I thought it reasonable. And, even before I returned the call to the doctor's office, I made up my mind that I would begin.

In 2010—after nearly a decade of my hard work—*Your Money & Your Life: A Guide to Building Character and Capital* was published. The feedback I got was that it was fantastic, but so varied in topics and filled with good information that it would've been helpful to be more subject-specific.

So, I went back to work for a few more years, and now you have in your hand the result—one volume in a five-book series called *Common Sense for a Prosperous Life*. One way or another, the writing of these books has taken much of my time for nearly eighteen years, and, at this moment, I still have no idea if this series will ever see the light of day. But I do know this much: books such as these are needed *badly*, and, if these books are ever published, everyone who reads them will be better off because they will finish every book with far greater clarity of thought for making decisions well that will determine the quality of their life.

Only a fortunate few are born into this world with a "wealth consciousness"—a mind that expects or creates wealth—or gifted with a highly marketable talent. The rest of us have to devote a great deal of our time to earning money and deciding how our very limited resources should be used. The Common Sense for a Prosperous Life series was written to give just this sort of reader a mature and sensible mindset toward all kinds of money matters, and also a blueprint for conquering our private demons and making personal choices that is as clear as "Follow the yellow brick road."

Let me begin by stating the obvious. For all but the truly wealthy, building a comfortable life will require several things:

- You must handle whatever you earn deliberately, so it does not slip away.

- You must earn more money than is required for food, clothing, shelter, and other living expenses (which, I admit, is increasingly difficult to do).

- You must not be careless with the money you save.

- You must overcome your own internal hindrances.

- You must not forfeit your progress to an undisciplined private life.

By the time you have finished reading this series, you will have a road map for the five "musts" above.

Book 1—*Riches Beyond the Bling: Clear Thinking on Money, Financial Independence and Life's True Riches* reveals how to handle the money you earn, purposefully.

Book 2—*Invest Like a Wealth Manager: Simplify Your Thinking to Invest Your Money with Confidence* gives you my own common-sense guidelines for saving and investing.

Book 3—*The Entry-Level CEO: Simple Secrets to Build a Profitable Business (Even with No Experience!)* is ideal for those with a desire to work for themselves. It relates some thoughts on increasing your income by building a business of your own.

Book 4—*Unchain Your Brain: Move Beyond Fear and Discouragement and Start Living with Purpose* delivers a powerful read for overcoming fear and discouragement and moving you toward your next goal.

Book 5—*Private Choices, Public Power: Personal Decisions that Determine Your Destiny* the fifth and final book in the series, is filled with practical help regarding personal issues, which, if handled carelessly, can wreck a life.

None of these books are a sermon, and they are not boring—I promise. I believe every page will grip you with its practical and immediate common sense. Pick up any of the books, open them anywhere, read three pages, and I trust you will not want to quit reading from right where you are. To my mind, that is the test of a well-written and worthy book: there is no place in it that does not quickly engage the reader on a personal level.

The lessons contained within are timeless. They will be just as helpful to a reader sixty years from now as today. So, if you are a parent and you can read this book without considering it imperative to set aside a copy for each of your children, I have failed. If you are a wife and you can read this book without insisting that your husband also read it, I have failed.

I truly believe you will not toss these aside: I am *that* confident that the five books in the *Common Sense for a Prosperous Life* series have no substitute in the marketplace. Having read hundreds of such books myself, I believe these are among those rare works immediately useful to every reader in every generation.

Welcome into my major life assignment, my best effort to make the world a better place by giving the reader practical instruction for the most important issues of life.

Choose well and prosper.

Mark Ashe
Gainesville, Georgia
2020

CHAPTER 1

TO BEGIN IS THE ONLY CHANCE WE HAVE

This was the most difficult of my five books to write. In these pages you will find thoughts that at various times helped me to keep going, though admittedly at times quite discouraged and uncertain. In your seasons of difficulty, it might be wise to return to *Unchain Your Brain* and browse its pages. It is likely that you will find a thought or two that speaks to you in that moment and strengthens you with surprising renewal of spirit.

Keep Thinking About It

This book is for the reasonably ambitious, for what Abraham Maslow called self-actualizing people: men and women who must be what they can be. If a paycheck and television are enough for you, I hope you feel differently by the time you finish reading *Unchain Your Brain*.

Like any treasure, our richest talents are not visible on the surface. You and I have gifts within us, but they must be mined. Like rubber bands, men and women are made to be stretched.

Your brain functions—or I should say, can function—like the servomechanism inside a torpedo's internal guidance system. Once programmed with a goal and launched, the "brain" inside a torpedo will, on its own, steer and course-correct to its assigned target.

Your brain has the capacity to perform this exact function for you. And it will perform this function when you speak to it in the only language the brain is programmed to respond to: an intensely emotional thought that is definite and that stays in your thinking.

I saw an interview with Elon Musk, the billionaire that started Tesla, the company that builds electric powered automobiles. He told the interviewer that in his college days he was on his first date with a girl and his first question to her was, "Have you ever thought about electric cars?" She said, "No, I haven't." He spent the entire date talking to her about electric cars. He added, humorously, "It was not a successful date."

We all move toward what occupies our mind. The more intense the thought, the more we *need* it, the more direct the movement toward it.

Despite the very real obstacles between you and your best life—and there may be many—as long as you can see yourself doing it, your brain is able to supply the way to it. However, the desire must be clear, and you must nurture it until it takes on a life of its own inside your head.

Let me say that another way, and I borrow this thought from Wallace Wattles, an early twentieth-century success author, though many of the great sages before and since have shared this same insight.

> ***You don't have to know how,***
> ***as long as you clearly know what you want,***
> ***and you want it badly enough to keep***
> ***thinking about it.***

Author and life coach Bob Proctor said it another way, "No one that ever did anything knew how they were going to do it. They only knew that they *were* going to do it." That is one of the most concise thoughts on the proper use of the human brain ever put into words.

This is not an invitation to rashness. I am simply pointing out that the obstacles, the unanswered questions, the unknowns and the "what-ifs" of life are endless, and if we think only on them, we will never live the life or make the contributions that we were intended to make. If there is a devil, then he wants us too doubtful, fearful or discouraged to reach for more. And the captious thought that we need to know how to get there does the trick most of the time.

One more thing before we move on. Without God in our worldview, the only explanation for our existence is randomness: the belief that we and all we see around us are the results of an unintended, unintelligent, and accidental chain of events that started when we were just polliwogs in a slime-pit billions of years ago. For me, that just takes too much faith, and at the same time, too little.

> *"Start where you are, with what you have. Make something of it and never be satisfied."*
> —George Washington Carver

Much in this book refers to God or directly to my Christian faith, but I am not writing to Christians, or at least not only to them. I am writing to people of all faiths—or of none at all. If you are of a different faith or subscribe comfortably to the idea of randomness, please apply the thoughts in this book in a way that works for you.

There are four main obstacles common to all of us other than the few that are truly exceptionally gifted. These are:

a) Fear of failure or of our own limitations in personality, mental ability, opportunity, actual skills, or the reality of current circumstances and the long odds against us.

b) Discouragement when we contemplate all that may be required, or later when on the journey, when facing the very real, seemingly insurmountable difficulties common to all upward journeys.

c) Too much reflexive attention to "facts" and obstacles and too little to possibilities and ways to take small steps forward.

d) Lack of understanding the power of the human soul, including your own, and therefore, a lack in clarity of intention despite all these very real facts and feelings.

I have and still do wrestle with all of these at times, and most likely so will you. This book, *Unchain Your Brain*, is the story of my all-too-common weaknesses and the little thoughts and victories that brought me through them. I hope it brings encouragement to you in your own times of testing.

CHAPTER 2
SELF-DOUBT AND FEARS

"The greatest gift you have is being right where you are, right now. Our fears are an important gift; to learn to walk through them, and in that experience to become whole ourselves."

—Response of a Near Death Survivor
when asked what she had learned from
her brief experience on the other side of life

was once in the presence of a national influencer and global personality who said he hated fear. He had battled it his entire life and still struggled with it. And yet, you can see him on television just about anywhere on the planet you may travel. Is he unusual? Of course not.

I know how hard it is to escape the mental whirlpool of worry and fear. For years, I was afraid my business would go under and I would not be able to find a job that paid a decent wage. I worried that if my business did collapse, I would not be able to provide for the needs of my family. All I had ever been trained for was being a policeman, and I knew we would struggle financially if I had to go back to that line of work.

Most distressing of all, after quite a few dismal years in business I began to doubt that I had whatever it was that enabled some people to succeed. That thought more than any other haunted me. I became so insecure and so fearful that I could hardly sleep at night. That's how much I dreaded each new day. And my fears were not without reason—things weren't going so well.

The business I found myself in was so foreign to my nature that it was hard to adjust to it. I was doing everything I knew to do, but, year after year, the parade of life just seemed to be passing me by while I was stuck making bricks without straw.

Despite all those years of exhausting effort, I just didn't seem to have the skills to build a life that was anything more than drudgery. My wife always supported and encouraged me. She was well aware of the price I was paying, and she was appreciative of it. But, true or not, I felt like a failure.

Most days I felt inadequate, embarrassed, and just plain tired of it all. I wanted a way out of the whole mess my life had become. All those dreary years were spent in a private torment I was unable to quell.

I can now tell you that the many difficulties I feared—even the things that seemed inevitable at the time I was worried about—never happened. But I suffered just as much, in fact more, than if they all had.

In truth, the fears I allowed to torment me were worse than whatever I was afraid of at the time, even had they happened. Why? Because if it happens, it happens once, and after you get over the shock, you start dealing with it and moving forward from there. But fear and anxiety are more sinister than reality. They take us through worst-case scenarios over and over again, day and night. There is never a resolution. The exhaustion we feel is not caused by our actual circumstances, but by emotionally living through dreaded outcomes again and again, scenarios that have not actually happened yet—and almost never do.

I worked for sixteen years in a business I could not escape and for which I seemed to have few natural gifts. I was worn away by the constant stress. I could see no way to make the job anything other than toilsome labor for a handful of bread; and finding a way to exit is very elusive when you are working to exhaustion every day. The real problems of each day were enough to tackle, but day and night—especially at night—I added to them the anxious thoughts my worried mind had on a mental loop.

Many times, my wife told me, "Mark, I understand your reasons for feeling the way you do, but no matter how certain these things seem to you now, none of it has happened yet, *and none of it is going to happen today.* Just do what you can now and give God everything beyond today." Fear is a self-induced mental illness. We can be given good counsel and know it is worth taking, and yet, be unable to stop our own mental self-destruction.

I am not complaining—though I have done my share of it. It is just a fact that most people will have seasons when things will be difficult, I have had mine and still do. My one redeeming virtue was that I would not quit. And let me tell you, when a man won't quit, he is hard to beat.

But let me say this again, my business and financial problems often looked unanswerable and inevitable.

However, not only did very few—or perhaps none—of the things I stressed over actually happen, but to my surprise, over time we prospered. Again and again, within a short time, I could barely recall the dilemma that had worried me so much just a few months earlier.

Jentezen Franklin, my pastor at Free Chapel in Gainesville, Georgia, preached a sermon in which he referred to this common overreaction as ANTS: Automatic Negative Thinking Syndrome.

Most of us suffer from ANTS in our minds to some degree. In hindsight, I can say with certainty that I have a very poor record when it comes to predicting the "inevitable," and I am sure you will find you are no better at it in your own life than I have been in mine.

If you and I kept a record of every time our rational mind told us to expect some dreaded outcome—and we tracked how often it actually turned out as badly as we feared—we would see clearly that we have a better chance of being struck by a plane falling from the sky.

> *The biggest lesson of my sixty-plus years regarding worry is that no matter what it looks like today, much or all that concerns us will have worked itself out by the time we actually get there.*
> —Mark Ashe

Many years ago, I began keeping a journal of events that made me fearful or worried and later noting the actual outcomes. I suggest you do the same. Within two years, reading mine became so ridiculous that it was only useful for a good laugh.

Money, or the lack of it, is one of our most universal worries. Once when I was stressed over a financial issue, I asked my close friend Armando Cartaya, who goes by his initials "AC," to have lunch with me. AC is as close as a brother to me, and one of the first people I go to when I need to get my thinking straightened out. AC and I are in the same type of business and have the same size families and similar obligations. During the conversation, I told him what I was worried about and then asked him how he kept himself from financial worry.

He said, "Mark, I'll give you a current example. I keep a folder that holds all the work that I have sold to keep my income going. I use it to manage my schedule. I know that when that folder is empty my income stops, but my bills do not. Right now, that folder is almost empty. I have only a few days of income left."

I asked, "What do you do to keep it from worrying you, AC?"

He looked at me very seriously and said, *"I just don't look in the folder!"*
We both laughed, then he continued,

When the income runs out—*if* it runs out—something will turn up or God will provide by some other means. I have lived for fifty-eight years, and I have never gone hungry or homeless, except maybe when I was a kid in Cuba.

I may run out of work for a while, but that happens to people all the time, and they survive it. What good reason can you give me for worrying right now, before any of this even happens? Why keep turning over in my mind imaginary scenarios and upsetting myself purposely? I have enough to take care of my family and me for today, no matter what may happen tomorrow.

He then looked straight at me and said,

Mark, you are worried because of things that you assume you can see coming. But no matter how likely they appear to be, they haven't happened. Not one thing you have mentioned has anything to do with something that is actually happening today or tomorrow or next week. You are opening mail that hasn't even been sent to you!

I learned the hard way that I am not in control of everything, even important things that naturally concern me. So I decided a long time ago to just "let go of the rope" and let God have it. I am not going to keep trying to hang on to the rope and save myself at all costs from everything that can or may ever happen.

I can try to control everything and hold on—until my strength gives out and then I free-fall to who-knows-where.

Or I can "let go of the rope" now and just trust God to catch me if I fall.

I have a wife and a family to keep up just like you do, and they know I am doing everything I can to take care of us. If trouble actually comes, we will handle it together as a family then.

I'm sure most of us who have struggled financially have thought, "If only I had more money, my life would be easy." I don't deny that money can make life easier, but it doesn't make it as easy as we think.

I have met quite a few wealthy men and women, and from first impressions when I was younger, their lives looked easy to me. But after I got to know a few of them well, this is what I learned:

- One of them had a daughter with bipolar disorder. The doctors could not get the medications right and the emotional swings were such a torment to her. At twenty years of age, she left them a loving note … then took her life.
- Another has only two children, and each has a different incurable medical condition that makes independent living impossible for the length of their lives.
- A third wealthy friend of mine recently lost his battle with cancer.

Given any choice at all, each of these multimillionaires would have tripped over furniture in a mad rush to trade places with you, even if your only earthly blessing is that you and your children are alive and well.

If they could trade positions with you and give you their money and take on your troubles in exchange for having their health and their children's health restored, they would do it faster than you could come to your senses—even if you are jobless, being evicted, and worried to a frazzle. And they would do it without a care in the world over what might come after that.

And even with the roles reversed, these folks who would give up their riches for health or the welfare of their children wouldn't worry about things like most of us do. Why? Because, based on what I have learned from them, they would take this attitude:

> If this money problem really comes at all, as long as I have my mind and my health, something will work out. Things never turn out to be as bad as they look in the beginning anyway. Never. I'll do what I can to prepare and prevent, but if it happens anyway, I have done what I can and I will figure something out from there.

How can I make such a claim, you ask? Well, a few years back I was in a dilemma that did threaten me with the loss of just about every material thing I had.

To calm myself, if only for a short time, I would go silently into my children's bedroom while they slept. I would look at them and think,

> If any one of these girls were diagnosed with a terminal illness and God said, "Give me everything you have built to date and everything you own. You will lose your home, your cars, your money, and your business tomorrow, but that child will wake up well in the morning," I would sign up before He had time to change his mind.

> I would go to bed and sleep like a baby and awaken giddy with lighthearted gratitude. My wife and I would go through the entire day without one concern about the financial losses or our future needs.

Can you have any doubt that a parent would see it this way:

"Well, we are starting over, but we are all healthy and together. Any God that can do this for us can figure out the rest of it, too, *This is great!* There is nothing at all to worry about now that our child is well."

The whole family would dance in the yard at sunrise without a single concern about anything material, all because one very sick child was made well. And yet, that happy scenario was far worse than where I stood in real life in that moment filled with so much dread.

Why? Because the reality was that all of us *were* well, and I had to face only the *possibility*—not the guarantee—of great loss.

I thought,

What a fool I am! That is exactly the situation where God has me now, all of us well and fed and sheltered for today. And he has only asked me to live with the possibility, not the guarantee, of a bad outcome in this matter.

Yet here I am, sleepless and worried, when I could give God some credit for being in control, even in this, and be grateful for all the blessings I do have, no matter which way this goes.

And, by the way, once again my wife was more sensible than I. She was not worried. She told me,

Mark, I understand the potential financial consequences for us, but I'm not going to let the devil buffet me with this all day and night. Just do what you can about it and leave the rest to God.

Give Him time to do what He does best, which is to make a way when there is no way. I don't care what the numbers look like or what the attorneys say. The Bible says that God daily loads us with benefits. Let's think about that rather than every bad thing that might happen at some point in the future. No matter what it looks like to you, God is working on this, and on us through it.

And God had me write this book instead of her? He does have a sense of humor.

Though I was too distressed at the time to take my wife's advice, I knew it to be true. And after two years of almost ceaseless anxiety, I ended up losing nothing but some money. Though that is never pleasant, it is a far cry from losing "everything."

Well, I did lose two years' worth of sleep—self-induced again, of course.

Then what right do I have to suggest that you not be fearful or worried in your next crisis? Well, who better to tell you where the shallows lie than he who has run aground on them? Here is what I hope I have learned and what I wish to share with you:

If you will quit fighting things that are not yours to control,
God will have the answer fall into place so casually,
it will seem effortless. God is always holding
the winning last hand for you.

You and I have no idea what is going to happen twenty-four hours from now, and I don't care what the summons or the lawyer or the judge or the banker or the registered letter says. Ninety-nine percent of the time, the thing that troubled us so much has worked itself out by the time we actually get to it, and the worst-case scenario is not even close to the actual outcome.

Stop Trying to Control What is Not Yours to Control

A few years ago, I talked with a lifelong friend, LaFonda Bruner, of Tulsa, Oklahoma. LaFonda was (and still is) dealing with life after a cancer diagnosis, and over dinner we were talking about the issue of facing the future without fear.

LaFonda told me,

> Mark, I am a control person. But this illness forced me to see that life—not just when troubles come—but *all* our life becomes a lot better when you let go of control. Controlling events is an illusion that we fight so hard to maintain.
>
> What is the sense of me praying and saying, "God, please help me. Please do this and please do that"? Probably He is laughing and saying, "Girl, I had this covered before you ever knew about it!"
>
> I should know that if it becomes necessary, He has the people in place to care for my children and comfort my parents. Sure, I want to live. But for now, I am forced to take the larger view that I will live whether it is here or there, and He has the details covered either way.
>
> We pray to God, but we don't really want to give control to Him. We just want Him to do what we ask. To put us at ease, we even want to see His solution soon after we pray. But when all control is taken from us, we finally see how foolish, and needlessly stressful on us, it is to live that way.
>
> Mark, I found out that this life is so much easier than I had ever allowed it to be. In fact, it is even easier now than it was when I had less to worry about but tried to control everything to suit myself. It's just a shame that we must

almost lose our life before we realize we have the opportunity in our own hands every day to start living it.

Thanks, sis. Is it any wonder that I love and admire you? I hope you are not concerned about more serious problems than this single mother with dependent children facing the possibility of a premature death. I know I'm not. So, the next time we are tempted to be fearful or worried, let's remember what Fonda taught me, even when dealing with a potential end-of-life diagnosis:

> He knew about this before I had it and has a plan to meet every need. My part is to let Him be God for me and quit worrying about ultimate outcomes. I will do what I know to do today to help, and then acknowledge His love for me and let it go. Besides, surprising outcomes are His specialty.

You might ask, "What if it has already turned out unfavorably?" If you did what you could to prevent it, then the way it has turned out is part of your journey. Take the new path and go forward with as much dignity and good cheer and strength of spirit as you can muster. Wallowing is for fools.

Odds are your life will not unfold as you anticipate anyway. But, if something you wish to prevent does occur, it is cheaper emotionally to let it happen and deal with it then, than to let the dread of it hover over your mind like a bird of prey for weeks or months.

In a Battle, Give Your Brain a Rest

Here is something that I learned in hindsight that will be helpful to you many times in your life. If you remember it, this will save you much emotional back and forth: If something has caused you concern for more than a few months, and you have not come up with a solution—*you don't have one. And all the thinking in the world won't change it.* In these cases, and I have had a few, it is better to leave it alone and deal with it if it ever happens, rather than lose one more hour letting it chew on you. Either it will never happen, or if it does, the unthought-of solution will appear right before or behind it. You can trust me on that one.

Though I was not always emotionally mature enough to practice this, I know from many needless distresses that it is actually smarter, and more productive, to let go of the fractious desire to "fix" everything that affects us. There are times that the best response is a resigned non-resistance:

If I can't control this or stop this,
If I can't get out of its way,
then letting it take over my life
for weeks, months, or years is pointless.
I need to just take the ride and let this work itself out.
Troubles always do.

I went through years of difficulties for which I had no answers. I prayed, and for years it felt as if no one was listening. But in hindsight, all was well. My life was being guided to good ends by wise hands. My wife told me more than once, "Mark, you have done what you can. And whether it seems like it's enough or not, it is all you know to do. So leave this alone mentally and enjoy the parts of your life that are not broken and let God deal with this in His own way."

She has always been proved right when it comes to matters of trust and faith. Sometimes the best way forward is just to let it go and let nature take its course. Sometimes the solution appears suddenly, and sometimes it is a gradual process. If we are praying for spring, we may have to wait out a winter, but in my sixty plus years, every time, the outcome was never the dreaded result that was expected. And it will be so in yours.

The accomplishments and the struggles of my life enabled me to write these very books and then live in perfect peace with the silence or success that follows their publication. When someone reads the words I write, even if it is fifty years from now, they will be able to prove it in their own life—because I lived it, and walked it, and proved it, before I wrote it. Our lives are not so different. The tough parts of your life have an unexpected purpose, too.

Let Go and Let God

During one time of difficulty, I remarked to a friend that I was reading the scriptures but not finding much to help me in my uncomfortable situation.

He responded as if I was an idiot: "The Bible was not given to you to help you understand your troubles, Mark. It was written to be believed. The whole message of that book is that God loves us, He knows what He is doing, and He is still in control, even when we aren't." Then he added, "What else do you need to understand?"

Once you have done all you can to resolve an issue, the only sane choice is to turn it over to God's ingenuity—and don't take it back. He will astound you with His effortless solutions. There is no other option anyway, except to let your mind grind you to powder. And what would that help, even if the worst did happen?

Besides, it is almost universally true that even the worst circumstances will eventually work themselves out. And you know what? If it weren't that way, life would grind to a halt because we are all fighting battles. So, if you are battling a fear of failure or poverty, or ill health, or anything else—and so many do—I urge you first to finish this book and then read Dale Carnegie's classic, *How to Stop Worrying and Start Living*. It is, perhaps, the best book ever written on the subject.

True Maturity

My friend, AC, had a period in his life when it was hard not to be discouraged. I wanted to know how he was holding up, so we arranged to meet for lunch. When I asked him to tell me how he was doing, he said,

> *"The trouble with most people is that they want to know the way and the channels beforehand. They want to tell Supreme Intelligence just how their prayers should be answered. They do not trust the wisdom and ingenuity of God."*
> —Florence Scovel Shinn

This is the hand I was dealt for now. God is not leaving me here, I know that. But for now, I am going to have to play the hand I was given.

The question is, will I approach this trial in bitterness or with the attitude that God can still be trusted, and He obviously thinks I can be, too?

I don't want to go my own way with my own solutions and find out five years from now that my own thing didn't work. Then I am five years older and a lot worse off. No. I'll play the hand I've been given and do it with a smile on my face.

I asked him to tell me what he did to keep his composure. He said,

Mark, I refuse to think about things that make me feel depressed or worried. I can't do anything about those things right now. I'm not going to look at the numbers and tell God what I don't have. I'm not going to upset myself by thinking about being in this position at my age. I have seen way too much good in my life for that, and God knows all those things anyway.

Instead, I will think about the promise God made to take care of us if we turn our life over to Him. It isn't my job to perform His promises for Him. It is His job to perform them for me. And I am going to rely on it, no matter what it looks like right now.

What else is there to do but worry and complain and tell all my troubles to anyone that will listen? How is that going to help me? No, I'll take it one day at a time and think about all the good things I do have: my loving wife, three happy daughters, plenty of food, and a warm home to sleep in tonight.

Sure, at times it is harder to do this as well as I would like to, but I am going to do it, no matter what. And to answer your question before you ask it, I'm sleeping just fine.

Mark, during a trial is our attitude going to be toward God or toward our own self-pity and complaining? I've been trusted with some weight on my shoulders for a season. That's nothing abnormal. Men are made for that. Now am I going to be a man here or not?

Wow! There is an example of a real man for you. Is it any wonder that I go to AC when I need my own attitude adjusted?

Of course, I have not always been able to live out AC's level of maturity. On one occasion, a friend who is a very successful businessman and whose judgment I value, kindly confronted me after listening to me explain my current business dilemma to him.

He said,

Mark, you are telling me what you don't have. When you spend your time telling yourself everything that you don't have, you are really just telling God what He can't do.

And you are limiting your ability to receive the answer. Remind yourself of all you do have and leave the solution to God. That turns Him loose.

His promises are not based on our resources, but His. I built a business that did $37 million a year at a twenty-percent profit rate. Do you think I figured all that out? No way! I did exactly what I am telling you to do here.

You said you have prayed about it and asked God for His guidance. Good. That's what I did, often. But then you have to stop letting human logic tell you how impossible it is. Take it to God and turn your brain off.

Let me ask you something. How ridiculous was it for a boy to bring Jesus two small fish and a little bread to feed five thousand men plus their families? Which facts could possibly make that make sense? No, the child just gave Him what he *did* have and left it there, and that was all he could do. It was God's business to take it from there.

When we give God whatever we *do* have and decide "I choose to trust you right now even though it doesn't make sense to me," there are no limits. Then, we need not concern ourselves anymore about the outcome.

Mark, we are not called to just talk like Christians, but to walk and live like Christians, and this is the process.

Record the Counsel of Wise Friends

By the way, I apologize for sounding as if I am preaching. Whether you are of a different faith or no particular faith at all, everyone needs friends who will confront their wrong thinking. With their consent, I often use a personal recorder to capture the most meaningful conversations with my close friends. Otherwise, I would soon forget ninety-five percent of their insight. No one can afford that.

We all have moments when pressures begin to take hold and reading scriptures or praying or whatever we normally resort to just does not help. That is when I listen again to my recordings of these valuable conversations with wise friends. As you can see, it can really be helpful later.

One of my personal counselors, a friend from church, is a woman decades my senior. I affectionately call her Miss Barbie. She was the personal assistant to a general in her early years, when not many women—much less women of African American ancestry—were given prominent roles in the workplace. My wife and I tell her that she is our adopted grandmother. When she speaks, you immediately realize you are in the presence of a remarkable person. When Miss Barbie talks, I listen.

During our last conversation, Miss Barbie told me something profound: "When you take your problem to God, you won't need to 'do' anything else about it unless He shows you. Just go on about your business normally and let Him work it out in His time and in His way. When the time comes, He just handles it." Then she snapped her fingers and said, "Like that."

She continued, "It is our troubles that make our lives rich." Some people, like Miss Barbie, just have the gift of rarely being fearful or worried because of their long experience in life. They have precious wisdom for us, if we will befriend them, assist them when needed, humble ourselves, and learn from them.

My aunt Bettye was also that way, and she had very difficult seasons in her life. She was the oldest of seven children, all born into a bare-existence home with an alcoholic father. She married a man who became an alcoholic himself: then, after he was paralyzed in a car accident, he tormented her with his jealousies. This led to her eventual divorce. By then,

Bettye had two daughters to raise alone, no money, and the need to find work.

I once asked her if she had ever worried. She told me,

Mark, most people make problems for themselves when they don't really have a problem.

You don't have a problem unless someone you love is dying, or your heart's not right with God, or your mind's not right. The rest of it just works itself out.

I never worried. If something bad happened, I would think about it that day, and if it was really bad, maybe the next day too. But I never worried about anything more than that. I just trusted God to figure it out and take care of me.

The Bible says that God will take care of us. I don't know where it is, but it's in there. It doesn't say that you will have the best of everything, but it does say that He will take care of us. You can find it in the Bible if you look.

I remember going to work without enough gas in the car to get me back home and having a twenty-dollar bill blow across my path in the parking lot when I was leaving. On other occasions, a customer would unexpectedly give me some money while I was at work.

I always had faith the Lord would take care of me. You should do the same. You and I don't have to figure out how, and it's best if we don't try.

Most of us are born with more of a worry/fear tendency than Bettye had. It may not be possible to reach her level of childlike trust, but let's at least consider Bettye's wisdom in our times of need and be guided by it: "You and I don't have to figure everything out, and it's best if we don't try."

By the way, she was quite poor, and after her divorce, had to move her young family in with her sister, my mother. Eventually she had to move back into her parents' modest home for years.

Later, after she had become prosperous—for several years in the 1980s she was one of the most successful real estate agents in the United States in sales volume—she was kidnapped and held at gunpoint while the kidnappers debated in front of her whether to kill her—and she told me she still trusted God, even in that, to take care of her.

Is There any Real Power to Help in Prayer?

If we choose to see our current problem as healthy and beneficial, as Miss Barbie said, we will immediately remove much of its power to harm us.

You may not be able to help feeling anxious at times, but you *can* decide that no matter what *may* happen at some time in the future, it makes no sense to live in fear of it today. How? By doing what my aunt Bettye did. Give the entire situation and all the possible outcomes to God. His ingenuity, even in "impossible" situations, is incomprehensible to us. But as Bettye proved over a lifetime, the ingenuity of God can be relied upon completely.

In my last truly serious crisis, I was struggling to apply this bit of wisdom myself—and not doing very well at it—when this thought came to me:

I need my next breath of air more desperately than anything that is troubling me right now. Nothing I am facing now is more urgently needed than my next breath. After all, if suddenly I couldn't breathe, everything I am worried about now would leave my mind immediately and be of no consequence at all.

My next breath is more vital to my survival than any-thing I have ever been fearful of or worried about—*and in my entire life I have never spent one minute worrying about whether the next breath will be there when I need it.*

So why shouldn't I "Let go and trust God" with these lesser things, too?

I remember another occasion when I was deep in thought over some serious pending difficulties. As I walked around my backyard praying, I noticed an insect struggling to stay afloat in my pool. I thought, "That bug's fate is sealed unless I intervene. Look at the futility of its struggle to escape. That bug is hardly a speck compared to the size of the problem it has. And it has no ability at all to even begin to imagine my power to casually provide the desperately needed solution."

As I bent over and let it climb into my hand, and then released it onto the earth, I realized, "God's ability to provide an answer for me is far greater than the difference between me and that bug. It took more of my energy for me to bend down and save that insect than it would for God to turn around all that concerns me, even though, if left to myself alone, there is no way." (I was advised months later that, without even informing me, a key person of authority had already favorably concluded my dilemma.)

Just as that bug, our understanding of *how* a greater power can reverse our situation, even at the last minute, or turn it to our benefit, *is not possible* for us. The solution that unfolds is usually completely beyond our capacity even to think of. And that is of no consequence at all to our complete deliverance and victory.

And I would add that from my own repeated experience, whether you feel any better after praying about it, and whether you see improvement or not, even for months, has nothing to do with your prayers being answered. Nothing whatsoever. I can say that because I discovered it from many such occasions over the course of my life.

What if you do not believe in the Christian view of God? The wisdom still applies. Many of the spiritual sages of history have recommended, and many medical studies have documented, the quantifiable benefits of prayer. Whether you are of a particular faith or of none, I still suggest you speak a prayerful blessing over the situation, close the prayer in grateful acknowledgement that you have been heard by the Almighty, and then, to the extent you can, "let go and let God." *We are not praying to air.*

The very morning that I am writing this is the beginning of a glorious spring day. I am sitting in a beautiful home, well furnished, looking at the flowers blooming just outside my window. My wife and children are fed and sheltered and happy. I could go on with my blessings. All this is true even though over the years I have spent many days deeply stressed over things I can't even remember now. In the end, they not only did not turn out as I expected, but I was being led to better things than I could see coming. The Bible calls them "green pastures." Here is my point: often things don't look so good before you get to those green pastures and still waters, but times of refreshing are coming. You will find this to be true in your life, too.

So, reader please, let me help you with decades of wisdom learned the hard way: Quit trying to figure out every angle of your problem over and over again. You aren't going to do it even if you stay awake twenty-four hours a day. Instead, let the power behind our complex universe work out your request with His reliable and amazing ingenuity. God created sub-atomic particles. No matter the subtle or complex intricacies of your need, solutions unfolding at the right time, solutions that you never could have thought possible or even imagined at all, will not tax Him in the least. Restful surrender is the worship that pleases Him most.

While hosting a swim party at our home for our daughters' friends, I had an enlightening conversation with a young mother in attendance whose husband had been killed suddenly in a motorcycle accident two years earlier. I asked her what she had learned in the intervening time. She said, "I learned I could have rested a whole lot more than I did. I learned I shouldn't have worried so much. I learned I didn't have to figure everything out. The stuff I worried about day and night for a year ended up taking care of itself without any help from me."

> *Most things we worry about just resolve themselves on their own. Most of the things we worry so much about are nonissues by the time they arrive.*
> —Tracy Ashe

I went to my dentist's office recently for a checkup. While waiting, I began a polite conversation with the dentist's new assistant. The wait was long, but as we enjoyed our conversation her story began to fascinate me.

Her husband had divorced her three years earlier. She lost her home soon afterward and she and her teenage daughter had to move into someone's unheated barn for a winter. She said that sometimes when they awoke in the morning, the water for washing was frozen on top.

I was stunned. I asked her how she had handled such staggering reversals over so short a period of time, and whether or not she had been worried sick. She said,

No. Early on I decided not to worry. I realized that whether I liked it or not that part of my life was over. My daughter and I were starting a new life with new conditions. I think after the initial shock wore off we both actually began to live with a curious anticipation. "You can't go down from here," we thought, "so what will today bring?"

Eventually, someone let us use a small heated trailer to live in, and working together, we got along okay. And you know what? My daughter and I are so close now, it is amazing. We loved that time together and we grew much closer to each other.

I realized I couldn't make my husband stay and he obviously was not going to. He had left me for another woman. I realized God was going to have to do something new for me now, and if I refused to accept this new season for me, I would only make myself miserable and drive everyone away.

Two years later, I met and married a man who does really well financially and who truly loves me. And he adores my daughter. I now live in the finest home I have ever owned. And I even got this great new job and I love it here. We are all truly happy.

Then, she offered me a bit of wisdom that ought to be cast in bronze in every home. She stated very matter-of-factly, "Mark, depression comes from fighting to keep things the way they are when God is changing them."

My pastor, Jentezen Franklin, is a practical man and that comes through in his sermons. One Sunday morning he spoke with the theme, "God's gifts come in strangely wrapped packages." His point was that God's blessings often look like setbacks when they arrive.

My new friend at the dentist's office accepted that she could not control the choices of another person, but she expected God's favor despite the injustice and the unwanted detour. She was led to a new place with love and material comforts. But that was after losing her marriage, her home, and spending a few months in a cold barn with her daughter. And it was during that detour that she and her daughter bonded with a new closeness and a special love that will last for life. But for her and all of us, it can sure look bad in the beginning—and stay that way for a while. It is God working out your life for good through it and after it that I am witnessing to.

Pastor Jentezen Franklin, Joel Osteen, and T. D. Jakes—all men of wide influence in the years this book is being written—were each so afraid of speaking before a crowd that in the beginning of their ministries they felt physically sick before preaching. But they stepped forward anyway, and they did it afraid. Today, all three are global powerhouses, more at ease when speaking to thousands than in anything else they do.

I used to dread going in to work because I was afraid others would see how unsure I was. But I did it anyway. Now, I own that business like a pet Collie. It provides many comforts for my family that would have been impossible for me to provide as a policeman.

When I was a policeman, I was worried about being able to provide well enough for my future family. Then, when I left to go into business, I worried that if I failed I would have no choice but to go back to being a policeman.

I never faced either of those scenarios, though they dogged me with anxiety for years. The things we worry about usually have nothing to do with today. Instead, they are suppositions about some apparently obvious eventuality—suppositions that almost always prove to be wrong.

If we will just live in today and refuse anxious thoughts about tomorrow, we will save our souls much needless wear and tear. Our tomorrows have already and will again repeatedly surprise us with favorable events. Sure, problems come. But in the end, much that is good comes into our life after them.

Today, I try to begin each day with this simple statement:

Something good is going to happen today!

And then I look for and celebrate even the slightest good thing. Gratitude is good soil for fresh favor.

Test Prayer as a Spectator

The next time you are in a spot of potential trouble, even if you are not particularly religious, try this experiment: pray for a solution and then watch the events as they unfold. But watch as a curious spectator rather than a worried participant—and see what happens.

Take the mindset of a scientific observer of prayer. When everything is concluded, if all is resolved satisfactorily, then acknowledge the divine help you received rather than dismiss the incident as a false alarm.

Too often we are like the man who prayed for a parking space at a crowded shopping mall and promised God that if he got one, he would start attending church. When suddenly a car backed out of a space immediately in front of him, he said, "Oh, never mind God. There's one now."

God may be invisible, but He is observably active on our behalf if we look for the evidence. When we quit dismissing His loving interventions as coincidences, we will begin to see the reality of His care for us. Seeing this, if we are wise, we will begin the journey of seeking Him in our decisions.

The truth is, apart from the severe illness or death of a loved one, most everything else in life will be set right after a little inconvenience. And honestly, I believe that even in the event of a parting due to physical death, the loss of our loved ones is made right again. The testimony of countless men and women, two of whom I have known personally, who have died for short periods of time and been resuscitated, have borne credible witness to life after life, as do the scriptures.

Every Choice has a Price

There is a price to be paid for living no matter what choices you make. Hiding from life has a price. Refusing to try has a price. Surrender has a price. Folly has a price. Success has a price.

You will not avoid problems whether you are trying to do something worthwhile or not, so do not be deceived into thinking that if you stay in your comfort zone you will get to avoid discomfort. No way.

In other words, when it comes to your life, my suggestion is that you might as well earn your stripes trying to accomplish something you really want rather than get beat just for showing up. Of course, do not be rash or foolish. Make the best choices you can. But don't let the self-doubts we all begin any new enterprise with—or the fear of uncertain outcomes—steal your best life from you.

I once received notice that a business arrangement I was involved in had become insolvent and I was liable for millions of dollars—which I did not have. This was way passed "might happen" and in the category of immediate fact. I could hardly eat or sleep for nearly two years. Yet, in the end, it was resolved without any of the dire consequences I had anticipated, even though after reviewing all the facts I concluded that there was positively no way out.

During this test, I was not wise enough or mature enough to follow this advice of doing what you can, then no matter how likely the result seems letting events take their course without allowing your worries to torment you every day. I lost two years of my life over something that in the end mattered very little. Life is precious, and exceedingly brief. There is no reason for us both to waste years of it fretting over outcomes we are no longer in charge of.

Having done what you can to be prudent and careful, if it goes wrong anyway let God have it and put your mind on the blessings you have remaining: family, health, food … the important simple things we overlook every day. Doing this is a battle, but it is good advice. There are times in every life when we must trust in something 'bigger than us' to sort out our mess for us. Don't keep beating yourself up. No one can foresee and avoid every problematic possibility. We all get smarter through some painful mistakes.

As much as you can, make up your mind that you will handle whatever comes up, *when* it comes up, *if* it comes up—and not one moment before. In the meantime, refuse to be fearful of things that have not even happened yet, may never happen, and if they do happen, may resolve themselves or lead you to a better place that you could not now remotely anticipate. Let me tell you from my own painful, borderline stupid experience: In time, this attitude will be justified in ninety-eight out of every one hundred issues that concern you— and those odds are not exaggerated.

Earlier in my life, I desperately wanted out of my home improvement business. God ignored my pleas for sixteen years, leaving me to struggle against an avalanche of discontents and dilemmas. Does that give the lie to everything I have said? Those were tough years, that's for sure. But it was during those years that I was made fit to write these books.

The very day I am writing these words, I am enjoying a blessed life that is more than I could even have dared to ask for back then—all because He left me right where I was. He had already answered my prayers for a better life, when I thought He was ignoring me.

I was afraid I would fail, and I felt that way for a long time, but I eventually built a good life, and I learned a lot in the process.

I was afraid I would lose my home due to my inexperience in business. Instead, as it turned out, I never missed a payment, and I now own four homes on my farm, all paid for. I began to think that I was missing something as a man—that I just did not have what it took to build a good life for my family—but did God put me at peace with that?

Well, *no.*

But it was that desperation which drove me to keep going when others would have quit and when I probably should have quit because I felt I had nowhere else to go. God in His wisdom did not allow me any other options because, though I did not know it, I was already on the right course. He had already provided the way, when all the while I thought He was indifferent or acting deaf.

Sometimes when we are begging for something better, God knows we will bloom right where we are if we will just stick to it. God may be silent during some tough years. He may instead prefer to see us *through* those tough years instead of removing us from them. But even if you are in that position, unless He tells you otherwise, He has scheduled unexpected transformations if you won't give up.

Don't make life-changing decisions when you're frustrated or in turmoil. Of all the fools in the world, the biggest may be the man who quits one job before he has another to go to. Of course, we may be talking about any number of issues other than your job, but you get the point. Until the way forward becomes clear, and you have heart-peace with it being best, stand your post like a soldier.

A Few Practical Insights for Navigating Life

The negative emotions we all battle at times—despair, anxiety, and fear—come from calculating events without giving God any credit in our asset column. If the Almighty called me home today and told me I could leave the most valuable lessons I've learned behind for my children, I might leave them a few thoughts something like this:

> Life is not a sugar forest for anyone, and it won't be for you. Between you and every goal is a garbage dump. You want the goal? Then you walk through the garbage.

Don't give your weaknesses so much weight in your mind. They don't matter nearly as much as you think. The most successful men and women I have ever known had plenty of surprisingly common faults and weaknesses not visible to the casual observer.

Persistence is indispensable to do anything worthwhile, and persistence alone will overcome a host of obstacles, including a lack of talent, specialized knowledge, or money. You can find or hire about anything you need once you start rolling, but you can't hire persistence. You have to bring that one yourself.

If you listen to all the reasons why something can't be done, you'll never do anything.

Thinking too far ahead is fatal to the pleasure of living. It causes most of our fears and worries. It kills initiative. And I have learned that it can't be done anyway. I am in a weather-sensitive business. I have watched highly skilled men and women predict the weather for forty years and I have learned this much: Any more than three days into the future, despite all their years of education, training, expensive equipment, and experience with forecast models—they usually have no idea what is going to happen *just 3 days from today!* And that will prove to be the case in your life, too. And with things far more important than the weather. Nothing is more changeable than "the facts." So don't waste your time trying to make provisions or plans too far ahead. You don't need to see the whole way there. You only need to take the next logical step.

We all overestimate the power of unexpected changes to harm us. Not once in my life has any scary, unexpected event turned out as badly as it first appeared. Not once.

Remember that when unexpected changes occur. And you might read Dale Carnegie's *How to Stop Worrying and Start Living*. I have found it helpful at such times.

It is important to avoid rash actions. Decisions, personal or business, made when very tired or very disgusted, made in haste or in anger, and important decisions that are made without counsel, can be the costliest mistakes of your life. Maintain relations with a few people that know you well and who can be depended upon for wise, common-sense counsel and use them. No one is wise enough alone.

The Bible says that the Wisdom that comes from above is pure. The way I apply that truth is that God's answer will be *clear when I see it*. Pure things are clear. Until you see clearly what to do and have heart-peace about doing it, stay still and delay decisions. When a glass has muddy water in it, if you set it down and come back in a few days, the water is crystal clear. The mud has settled to the bottom. The water is so clear you can read through it. When I'm unsure, I'm in unsettled water. I say to myself over and over "Wait *until the water in the glass has settled completely and is clear*."

Here is another bit of wisdom that will save us from quite a few blunders: Don't make commitments or decisions until you must. A thousand things can change. Wait to make commitments and decisions until it is time to make them.

If you decide to go into business or take any kind of calculated risk, avoid putting yourself into a position where you will be ruined if it does not work. Here are a few thoughts on how to decide whether to start a business or change the course of your life in a major way:

1. Were you born with a passion for doing something that can make profits? That one's a no-brainer! It's in you!

2. Did the events of your life open this door naturally or are you forcing it because you want it to work?

3. Is there an idea that keeps gnawing at you for months or even years that will not go away even though you keep trying to make it go away? That's one to pay attention to.

4. Has there been an unexpected thought of crystal clarity that inspires you to toward decisive action? Something you can just "see" so clearly? Those events are rare, but they do happen, and they are important to our future. Act.

Don't resist everything you don't like. It's too emotionally costly. If some situation or person disturbs you, but you can't change it or avoid it for the time being, then stop cursing and resisting it. Instead, bless the situation and the people involved. Non-resistance makes room for it to pass. Just say an audible prayer, "I bless these people and events. At the right time they will leave my life and be turned to my good."

When I give people a gift, I want them to enjoy it. The purpose of a gift is to give pleasure to the one receiving it. Our life is a gift from our Creator. He wants you and me to learn to *enjoy* it. A clear conscience allows that. Conscience is the spiritual faculty that keeps us connected to our Higher Power and on course for our best life.

As the years pass, your time here, in the end, will seem brief. Be wise. Enjoy the journey. Don't wait for things to be different or better. It's always a mixed bag of difficulties and blessings. Acknowledge and enjoy the good you have now.

Think in Small Steps and Let Others Use Their Gifts to Help

During the writing of this book, I have repeatedly had to push back against the thought that I was wasting my time. How could I write a book and make it interesting? I had never written anything. My own mind repeatedly told me that any book I might write would not be worth reading and would never be published. And common sense told me that, even if it were published, the odds of an unknown person writing about money, running a business, living life to a purpose, success in marriage and other private choices—and then having the books come to the public's attention—were about zero.

> *Thinking will not overcome fear but action will.*
> —W. Clement Stone

But I learned in the building of my first business that self-doubts and discouraging thoughts and all the very real facts that support them are an inseparable part of every success story.

In other words, I learned how to endure discouragement without being deceived by it. This very day, as I sat down to write, the improbability of what I am attempting to do came heavily over me. *I ignored it.*

Every man or woman who has done anything worthwhile has had to step out despite his or her own fears and doubts. I have learned that my job is just to heed that inner witness of what I should be doing and then find a way to step toward it.

In fact, when this book is finished, I am considering another venture: to market a chili I make. I have no qualifications at all to market a food product. The thought feels like foolishness even as I write these words. So, let's talk about that in order to highlight a few points that may benefit you with your goals. (By the way, if any of you readers are successful in the food manufacturing/distribution business, please contact me. I would value any suggestions you might offer!)

Just about everyone who has tried my chili says, "That is the best chili I ever ate!" Friends constantly ask me to invite them over when I make it. They tell me they will gladly pay me if I will make it for them. And they are sincere. I *know* it could sell.

But I also know there are a thousand obstacles to overcome, particularly for someone who knows absolutely nothing about the business of food production, packaging, and distribution. Whenever I think about all that would be involved, a daunting awareness of the odds against success fills my mind.

So, if I decide to do it, I simply won't think of it that way. I know ahead of time I can't win against those thoughts. They are too legit and too many. So, I will not think about permits and purchasing, manufacturing and distribution, shelf life, and management—or any one of a thousand other obstacles that haven't even occurred to me yet.

Instead, should I decide to step forward, I must shrink my objective down to terms my mind *can* handle. If I feel led to begin, I will set a goal to find someone experienced to make and sell the minimum-sized commercial kitchen order of chili *one time only*, and then quit and never do it again.

Already that feels very different, doesn't it? Who couldn't survive that? Once that is done, I will see what I have learned and then decide if I want to do anything beyond that.

It may be naïve of me to assume even that small step. But, if I feel led to move forward, I will find some first step I *can* take without feeling overwhelmed. If the Spirit speaks, and keeps speaking, I am willing to listen without killing the dream before a single step is taken. That is all I am saying.

If a few years from now—or tomorrow—an inspired idea comes into your heart that possesses you against the odds, as inspired ideas usually do, I hope you do the same.

Most of us never give our dreams a chance because of the odds. But those doubts come from attempting too much mentally. By shrinking the size of the task in your own mind to only one manageable step, you minimize the obstacles. And the reasons against acting on the thought instead of just thinking about it get smaller.

After you take your first step, if you choose to go on, the size of the tasks you can take on will increase naturally based on what you have learned so far. And if you find you wish to continue—and remember, no rule says you have to—the fears will gradually melt away and be replaced over time with new skills. And a new skill repeatedly performed becomes a new level of competence, and competence results in self-confidence. No one starts out knowing what to do.

In fact, there is no reason to even think in terms of long-term goals or outcomes. In the beginning when thoughts are forming new ideas, it is far too soon to be tackling those things mentally. It is not going to unfold like you planned any-way. You just need to move forward *a little*. Just pick some small step to take and make that your only objective. Just take one logical step each day and see if that helps shed some light on your path.

> *Dare to be wise; begin.*
> —Horace

If you survive that—and you will as long as you don't take a tall dive into shallow water—you can decide what to do from there. Keep it "doable" in your mind.

The courageous daring to begin, to step out on your own ideas, to consider your thoughts to have as much merit as anyone else's, to take one small step at a time in the face of an uncertain outcome, is the most basic determinant of every success story in the world. If you want to live your own success story one day you must quit mentally sparring with your dreams and take a step forward. You will never do that if you mentally take on the whole journey at once.

My last suggestion on this subject is the one that, to me, has the most power to liberate us to act. I discovered it from Dan Sullivan. Dan is one of the nation's top business coaches (strategiccoach.com). Dan said the reason that people procrastinate is because when anyone considers a new goal, the first thing we all ask our self is "How do *I* do this?" That question is what causes us to procrastinate. But Dan points out that that question is the wrong one to ask. The correct question is, "*Who* is the right person to help me do this or, even better, to do this for me?" Dan said we need to be seeking for and connecting with the right WHOs to get it done, not thinking about the HOWs.

Dan Sullivan and Dr. Benjamin Hardy teamed up to write the book, *Who Not How*, to explain this principal of team building. I encourage you to pick up a copy. As an example of the *Who Not How* concept in practical application, I wrote my books, but someone else is doing nearly everything else. I am not bogging myself down trying to learn new skills. Yes, I am paying them for it, but if it all depended on me it would never get done. I lack too many of the technical skills. Fortunately, my daughter, Saige-Remington, is on my payroll and she is able to do much that I cannot.

Specialized knowledge is one of the most easily purchased commodities on earth. Men and women that do something well enjoy doing it, and they like getting paid for it, whether part-time or full-time. Skilled people are not nearly as expensive as the wear and tear you will put on yourself trying to learn new skills that only frustrate you. I paid someone to help me with book titles, design the covers, build a website, and a hundred other things I did not want to do. And I did each step only as I could afford it. Speed was not my concern. Getting a first-class product to the market was.

The Journey Corrects the Flaws

Here are a few more thoughts to help you act on your inspired ideas.

I have learned from scripture and from experience that God's ideas for us are big things that we cannot do without Him. I have never known of a single exception. God wants us to do new things, discover our unrealized talents, and get to bigger rewards. It is in the doing of the thing that we learn to rely upon Him. That is why so often flashes of divinely inspired ideas will come with a feeling of logical absurdity. Even today, we still must choose if we will eat from the Tree of Life (inspired guidance) or the Tree of Knowledge (our current experience, understanding, and skills).

And please, I must assume in the reader enough maturity not to mistake every flight of mental fancy as a divine idea. The true inner witness will come from the heart, not the head. It will feel incongruent to our knowledge and skill and will not leave us alone though we repeatedly dismiss it as absurd.

And here is a second helping of encouragement for you: even very successful people have common faults and feet of clay.

I have made the acquaintance of some very wealthy men and women. And you know what I found out after I came to know them? From a distance, we overestimate them. Greatly so. They are just like us, but with one exception: they learned to do one thing well that pays a good bit of money. In every other respect, they are quite like you and me. That should encourage us all. I found out that the big shots were just little shots that kept shooting.

You and I don't need to become some gifted business guru. All we need is to do one thing so well that others will pay us for doing it. Right now, (and until you get a few millions of your friends to buy one of my books), I repair homes. It's not glamorous. It's not going to put me on the *Forbes Magazine* list of the world's richest men. It's just what came to me on my life path.

But after beginning it with great uncertainty, and doing much of it poorly, I learned to do it well enough that I have attained a very comfortable life from it. We use what life gives us and build on it.

Yes, I wish someone had offered me a path to a corporate presidency, but it didn't happen. So, we answer our fears with enough faith to take a step forward. Confidence comes along after stepping into the current that is moving in the general upward direction we wish to go.

You can't cut something so thin that it doesn't have two sides. Uncertainty and confidence are just two sides of the same coin, so quit waiting for a one-sided coin to show up. You don't get one without the other. You develop your capabilities while on the journey.

Do you want there to be more to you as a man or woman? Do you want to become more capable and confident? Do you want more money? Then you pick up the coins God puts on your path and you don't squabble about which side is face-up at the time.

I once asked a wealthy elderly gentleman how he had become so successful in a business where almost no one makes money. He said, "Every time a bigger door opened, I stepped through it."

Everyone Has Deficiencies

We are all far too conscious of our weaknesses. We give our weaknesses way too much weight in our minds.

Consider this. The Chinese are famous for championship Ping-Pong. Years ago, I watched the coach of a world-class Chinese team being interviewed. The interviewer asked, "What do you do to overcome the weaknesses of your players?" The coach replied, "We pay no attention to a player's weaknesses. We concentrate on developing his strengths until the weaknesses are unimportant."

All of us are deeply flawed. That disqualifies you from nothing. Find one thing you can learn to do well—something people will pay you to do—and concentrate on becoming an expert at it. Cut the mental chain to your imperfections loose. They are there, just as mine are, but they will not disqualify you from anything you are willing to learn to do. Yes, it should be our intention to grow and improve our skills and character. But it is the journey, the desire for more, the upward reach, that will wash away so many of our faults.

Your shortcomings don't make you one bit less of a person than the most accomplished men and women you admire. Those people are the same as you and I. They are good at one thing but flawed in many other ways. We can all become our own version of them. In the end, the various flaws common to us all won't matter at all if we learn to do very well whatever we do.

CHAPTER 3
THE DECEPTION OF DISCOURAGEMENT

The classic American Christmas movie *It's a Wonderful Life* begins with a conversation between God and an angel with the unlikely name of Clarence. The angel is being dispatched to earth to assist a desperate man. Clarence asks God, "Is he sick?" God replies, "No, it's worse than that—he's discouraged."

We all are downhearted from time to time, but when discouragement runs on until we begin to think that things will never change for the better, it can drain all hope away. I have had that unfortunate experience.

That type of complete despair infected me for less than a year, but that was more than enough to prove to me that we toss the word "hopeless" around far too casually. If a true state of hopelessness is ever reached, a breaking point is not far away. Humans are not designed to live without hope that something better is at least possible.

All of us—whether we believe in a spiritual dimension to human life or not—are going to face issues over which we have no control and for which we have no answer. If you never have to go through one or two of those dark episodes, you are in a very small minority.

When we feel lost and desperate for long enough, even the most adamant agnostic may turn to prayer. So, if you will once again excuse a reference to my own faith, I will share how I outlasted my seasons of doubt and disillusionment.

In addition to my brief period of hopelessness during which it felt as though my life had little chance of improving, two other times I faced unavoidable long-term struggles that seemed unanswerable. Like air slowly leaking from a tire, discouragement that drags on long enough will cause us to believe the verdict is final. But of

> *The biggest thing I learned is to just keep putting one foot in front of the other until things turn around.*

course, that's not true. There is always the possibility of a completely unexpected breakthrough. If you are going to make something out of your life, odds are pretty good that you are going to have to endure periods of discouragement without being beaten by it.

To be frank, the biggest thing I learned is to just keep putting one foot in front of the other until things turn around. If you don't go *through* the hard times, you can't get to the good times. And that is true in business and marriage and mistakes with money and just about anything else worth having.

In hindsight, one of the most surprising things I learned was that my faith in God was not anything like I had supposed. When you can see no way for life to change for the better, and when months drag into years … well, hearing that God still has a way to take you to a great place feels like asking an adult to believe in fairy tales.

But this is important for you to know: God is not offended. His plan for us is not changed by our disillusionment and bitterness in such times. The good things you are bereaved of for now are still in your future. My assurances won't amount to much when you're so emotionally distressed that you are fighting for air to breathe, but it's true, nonetheless. And I learned it from real life, not from reading a book or hearing a motivational message. Here are two strong resources that are vital in a battle: first, you need to *cling to* your spouse if they have more faith than you; and stay in your house of worship. Those two pillars of emotional support can keep us upright when alone we would suffer a complete loss of will. If there is a devil, then like all predators when he is moving in for a kill, he wants to get you off by yourself. Stay connected to your spouse and your house of faith.

I did many regrettable things during those tough years. I complained to my wife, I moaned, I worried constantly, I lost sleep, and in my heart, I accused God of criminal negligence. But— and this is important—I did not quit working! I did not quit being a husband and father. I did not quit showing up for my life just because I felt desperately unhappy and hopeless. I had responsibilities, and as long as I could put one foot in front of the other, I was going to keep going.

Of course, had a better option been offered to me, I would have taken it. But none were, so I kept plugging away where I was. And if I had quit, or turned to alcohol or drugs, or closed myself off from the world, I would have let the devil of despair do exactly what he came to do: stop me right where I was.

There are seasons in the lives of most achievers—and for that matter, most everyone—when the loss or denial of important things that we really want seems to loom over us. Especially when you want for something more than a normal day-to-day life.

The Bible promises "[W]ith God all things are possible," and that leaves *nothing* out. It is hard for a human to get their mind around a claim that large, especially when their tank is empty. To believe those words under dire conditions, is a test that few will pass. Fortunately, it won't be held against us. The trial passes and we are still protected and promoted. In my experience, we get a passing grade just for finishing the test.

What does "with God" Mean?

I own a home improvement business, and I am good at it. If I offered you a chance to start a similar business with me, the fact that you know nothing about it would not be nearly as important. If you go into business with me, the odds of your success will be greatly increased, even if all I ask you to do is answer the phone. You don't have to know much if your partner knows a great deal more than you.

The decisions I make may seem to be a mistake at times. But, if you are in this business with me, you can just keep doing the simple things I ask of you each day, even when what is happening does not make sense to you. Why? Because you already know that as your very skillful and successful partner, I know what I am doing but you don't. You can just do the things I ask of you, like come into work tomorrow and answer the phone, and rely on me to "get us there."

That is exactly what the words "with God all things are possible" means. Not "*to* God all things are possible." Who would argue with that? The word is *with*.

When the way forward feels nearly impossible, here is Lesson One:

Don't stop showing up for your life.

When you get up and put one foot in front of the other, even in a mental state that feels devoid of interest, it is a victory for that day.

Just do the normal things you can do each day, and do them without much thought—and keep showing up.

And here is Lesson Two: **Stop relying on yourself.**

If you had the solution, you would be doing it. You can condemn yourself and resist everything around you or you can just take the ride and let go of the heavy end of the log. When the way forward is presented, it will just appear and make sense. That is when we experience the reality of the words "with God."

Now we all want to know when breakthroughs are coming: "But when will God move on the need? How long will this disheartening waiting game take?" Those answers, unfortunately, He reserves to Himself alone. And that's tough to take, especially if several years have passed and more of the same is all that seems to be ahead for you. I went through that scenario the wrong way and we don't both need to make the same mistakes. If an attractive alternative is offered, one may consider it, hopefully with prayer as well as counsel and reason. But if not, what choice is there but to either quit or do our best where we are while we await some positive change? Which one makes the best sense to you? The question answers itself.

My two biggest turnarounds came after I was completely empty. As far as I could see, there were no answers, and I had no more will to seek them. I had surrendered emotionally to whatever happened. I had finally arrived at the strange paradox of working each day, but in complete, impassive non-resistance, not out of wisdom, out of exhaustion. I have a few times come to the strange place where, all hope being lost, I let go completely and experienced absolute peace with nothing externally different. And in that state, solutions effortlessly appeared. I was unable to do this as an act of will, but if you can, get there and stay there. That is miracle ground! There is always a way for good things to happen, if we keep getting up and getting dressed and showing up for our life during the dark seasons.

Non-Resistance: The Key to Emotional Survival

I was discouraged when I could see only more drudgery after years of effort in business. But my business didn't fail as I expected it would, and I was totally debt-free by the age of forty-six.

My marriage didn't fail due to the stress either, even though from time to time there was quite a bit of it. In fact, ours became the best marriage I have ever known of. For years I privately berated myself because I was married to a wonderful woman and while other men I knew were making much of their opportunities I struggled to provide for us. I secretly felt as though Tracy, with her beauty and character, could have married the president of a global company, but instead was getting less than she deserved from me. She never thought that way at all. I was just discouraged.

But as it turned out, I was not as incompetent as I felt. There were indeed great things in our future, things I had absolutely no way even to suspect were possible, and I believe there still are.

I once asked my brother-in-law how he managed to go from one of the most distressed people I had ever known to one always at peace with his life. He said,

> I nearly let despair and stress over money kill me. When I think of the years I wasted, dreading the next day, I can't believe I lived like that for years. I once actually held a gun in my hand and debated ending it all.
>
> I finally decided that if I couldn't fix it, then I should just let God take care of it, no matter what happened to me. I don't know how many days I have left on this earth, but none of them are going to be filled with anxiety and despair over stuff I can't fix anyway. The devil has had all the fun with me he is going to get on that account.

I have always remembered one phrase he used that really struck a chord with me—and I have found it to be an effective way to deal with life. He said, "Mark, just let God work His magic."

I have used some variation of his words of wisdom to calm myself more than once, and whenever I can live up to it, it truly helps. Here is a sample of a good "talking to" with myself:

My anxious mind is not helping me at all. In fact, its only making it worse. I have done what can and I am going to let God have it. And no matter what happens after that, I will live with it. His hands are bigger than mine and I'm leaving it there.

Sometimes the smart play mentally is just to relax, show up, and "answer the phone when it rings."

When we are in a tough spot desperately sifting through the facts over and over is an exhausting waste of energy. You won't get the answer that way. If your head had the answers, you would already know it. But when we are discouraged, our reasoning mind sends us again and again onto a hamster's wheel of detail-sifting and worry. It is pointless. Most of our suffering is caused by a worried mind allowed to run wild on its own.

> *It's a great life ... if you don't reason.*
> —Florence Scovel Shinn

I have done it both ways:

1. stewed and worried and worked my mind to exhaustion
2. simply let God have it and see what happens after that

The second one works a whole lot better. Admittedly, at times I was not as good at it as I wish I could have been, but it *does* work, and it works *A LOT* better.

God is not like us. He does not need different circumstances or more favorable facts to reverse our situation and even turn it to our benefit. He does not need us to be more talented. He needs us to quit reproaching ourselves. He does not need *anything* but our trust and surrender. In a dilemma rest is true worship. In such times, our degree of rest in Him is His degree of pleasure in us. Do whatever is obviously helpful, then turn it over to God. In a trial, the degree of our trust in Him will be the degree of His pleasure in us.

What if Bad Things Do Happen?

I know what you may be thinking: that sounds good, but very undesirable things do happen. What then?

Let me share with you what my wife told me once when I asked her that same question. We were in financial difficulties, and I was not sure we would even keep the home we were in. I asked her how she felt about it.

Tracy said, "I am going to believe God wants us to keep our home. But even if we don't, I do not expect either one of us to be upset about it. It just means that God has something better for us on the other side of this test, whether we live here or somewhere else."

That is true maturity, emotionally and spiritually. She was determined not to be dominated by fear. People lose their homes every year and everyone lives through it. Yes, bad things do happen—not nearly as often as we think they may—but they do happen. But if we refuse to wallow around in pity over our losses, that will not be how our story ends.

Just recently, my wife and I stopped helping a woman for exactly that reason. She has quit trying to help herself because of past disappointments. When encouraged to get back to work and get back to her life, she just starts recounting all her losses. She lives off her aging mother and refuses to help herself. She does little-to-nothing to instruct and guide her sixteen-year-old daughter. And she defends her condition by rehashing all that happened to her in the past. There is no way to help someone who chooses self-pity.

Yes, she has had disappointments, betrayals, and financial reversals. But she refuses to step back into her own life and live it. Christ said to such people, to paraphrase in my own words, "Turn away from your past and your losses and follow Me. I have come to lead you to a more abundant life. Stop looking backwards. Let the dead bury the dead."

In other words, keep putting one foot in front of the other, one day at a time, and give God something to work with.

A positive attitude does not mean we expect everything to turn out as we want it to. It means that, just as my wife demonstrated to me in our times of testing, we are restful and expect to be okay no matter how things turn out. That is the healthy way to deal with real life. That is how we walk on top of troubled water. That is character and courage and grace in action. "I will be okay no matter which way this goes."

Non-Resistance

As I said, my own breakthroughs were dramatic, and came after I stopped fighting to control events.

I stopped resisting everything—not from wisdom, as I should have—but out of complete demoralization. I no longer had enough faith in God to even ask for help. Maybe once I quit resisting and complaining my negative energy was finally out of the way? I don't know. But I do know that soon after letting go of any thought of control, a remarkable and unexpected infilling of mental and emotional power came into my mind, and I was literally free. I had a new mind with full confidence in my own abilities, and I soon began to move forward with authority.

I was so amazed at what was happening that it seemed as if I were watching from a distance. I was in a state of wonder as I observed the clarity and authority of my new thought processes. The business conundrums, formerly so perplexing to me, now seemed inconsequential compared to my ability to meet them.

If mental states could be quantified like a physical healing, it would have been a measurable miracle. It felt like I had my own resurrection. What happened was, in fact, exactly that. Suddenly I knew what to do—and I knew that I knew it. Doing business well and profitably became automatic, the strain on my marriage disappeared, and in the next few years, my income grew by many times what it had been. But the new 'me' was the real gift.

Which of us when in despair can anticipate that such miraculous transformations are coming? No one. But I have seen it in my life and in the lives of others, many times.

> *The instant you ask,*
> *Infinite Intelligence knows*
> *the way of fulfillment.*
> —Florence Scovel Shinn

We all go through tough times, but there does come a time to stop our determined resistance. Non-resistance does not mean hopeless surrender to defeat. It means that after doing our part each day we accept the fact that in life there are seasons when it is not our turn to "drive." Being human means that there are times when we aren't in charge. And even when we are powerless or completely lost, there is One to Whom we can turn that is neither. When it looks bad to us and we can't change it fast enough—or at all, it's time to let forces bigger than us have it.

As long as we have breath there is hope. We all have heard of irrefutable accounts of miraculous healings of the body. Who can deny that other miraculous events of every sort happen every day all over the world? Miraculous transformations in mental health, relationships, business deals, money, legal matters and release from addictions do happen, every day. Probably millions of them. Wake up, clean up, suit up, stand up and spit in the devil's eye.

In other words, to think there is no way out of our mess, and no hope for our future, is total nonsense!

A few tough years when our circumstances feel wrong and depressingly permanent are normal for the great majority of us at different points in our lives. Sometimes our life is not a race to a prize, it is a struggle for mental poise.

Aimee Copeland (aimeecopelandfoundation.com), a beautiful twenty-something young lady who had lost all four limbs to an infection and went forward to make much of her life, told an audience I was in, "When all seems lost it is important to remember that there is a greater plan currently happening above all of that. It is simply hidden from our sight behind the dreary days. Don't hang on to the dark emotions. Let them pass. Good things are still coming." That was my experience, too, and with far lesser challenges. That can be your story if you let go of the determination to control every outcome, give God a little room, and keep showing up for your life.

The wise Chinese have a proverb for the tough seasons of life: *Leave your cuff to the tailor.* That means there are times to just let God bring you to the right place, plan, or people by His own inscrutable path.

In waiting times, uncertain times, and in hard times, don't resist everything you don't like. If you can do something about it, fine, do it. If not, bless the situation when it comes to mind and let it take its course. Give God a little room to "work His magic." When everything looks like it is going to fall down anyway, maybe the best choice left is to just let it fall and see what new thing God has for you. As my dental assistant explained, fighting to keep things as they are when God is changing them is what leads to our distresses. Trust the ancient wisdom of the Orient. When you can't stop it, avoid it, or change it, then "leave your cuff to the tailor." It is amazing how often it is just a new promotion arriving in a strange package.

One Call, One Chance Meeting, One Unexpected Event can Change Everything

The following story was related to me as a truthful occurrence, and it is certainly plausible. True or not, it does demonstrate how casually God can do that which we consider absurdly impossible, so I will repeat it here.

The story is set in the coal-mining region of the Appalachian Mountains in the eastern United States. Too many years have now passed for me to remember the town and the dates and names, but all were given at the time this story was told to me.

A man had died, leaving his son to inherit a mountain across the road from the home where the boy still lived with his widowed mother. The young man, a rather rustic and uneducated lad, decided he wanted to build a church on the land, but the mountain standing on that spot made that impossible. He needed a level lot.

He found in the Bible that, if he had faith he could "say unto the mountain, Be thou removed," and it would be removed. (Mark 11:23, KJV) He told his mother he was claiming that verse. His mother explained that the verse was not meant literally. It was a figurative statement about the mountains we face in our life. But he would not be dissuaded.

Now, let me ask you, what are the odds of that prayer being answered? Is God able to remove a literal mountain that has stood on that spot since countless eons before human history?

These people did not have the money to pay for the project, nor would ten lifetimes of labor have been enough for the task. And in fact, the young man had no intention of doing anything—other than asking, and waiting.

Is not this prayer foolish and the request impossible to the point of absurdity? I would say so. Can God remove a mountain? Can God answer our prayers when what we are hoping for is quite impossible?

The answer is, "Yes. And casually."

A few weeks later, three men showed up at the door of this woman's home and asked to speak with her son. They identified themselves as representatives of a company working a pit mine a few miles on the other side of that mountain. The mine had played out of ore, but the laws of the state required that the pit be filled before they could withdraw. They needed fill material, and a lot of it!

Their engineers had surveyed the region and their computations showed that this boy's mountain contained the amount of rock and earth they needed.

They wanted him to sell them the mountain.

They did not want the land it sat on—just the ancient, worn Appalachian mountain that had stood there since before humans walked the earth. They offered to pay him to *let them remove the mountain*, and they would leave him the level lot that remained. He agreed, and built the church with some of the proceeds.

No matter how lost or hopeless we feel during a particular season of our life—God is, and He is aware of our need. Based on my own experiences, I can no longer doubt it. He can do casually what all our reasoning and logic declare is not possible. No matter how desperate and dire the facts, that does not constrain God in any way. Not at all. Never. Not one bit. There is always an answer.

The candid truth is that most of us do not believe this. We all understand what the words mean and think we believe them, but to rely on that truth when in a deep trial for which we have no answer, well it is simply more than most of us can grasp in the moment. We cannot get to God's level, so in our times of need we tend to pull Him down to ours when considering what is possible. We think we believe in God, but our real opinion of God is revealed when what we need is impossible, when only a *real* God will do. What we sometimes discover is that we believe God can do more than we can, He can help when it's not too big, but not when it is "impossible."

I went through that test a time or two and failed it. But God didn't. He graciously rescued me anyway. Sometimes from the dilemma, sometimes through it, but always the outcome was more favorable than I thought possible during the fight.

Look, I don't claim to have all the answers and I don't know why many have truly difficult struggles. But after underestimating God for many years, I do know this: God loves us, and

He knows what He is doing even when we don't like it one bit. He can do the impossible casually when we just let Him have His way. When you release your cares because you have confidence in the love and character and ingenuity of another person, it is called faith. Who better to help than the only One who is not limited in channels, methods, means, or money?

An Effective Way to Deal with Discouragement

The sobering reality is that very few of us will get through our lives without going through a serious trial of some kind, and most of us will go through several. So if you are going to endure discouragement and come out on the other side and go on toward your desires, you must have some way to fight back. You must have some way of picking yourself up and getting back to work in earnest when you feel discouraged or defeated.

I have a dear friend, Bobby Dollar, who is a millionaire businessman and a delightful gentleman. (Isn't that a great name for a millionaire?) Bobby, who is now along in years, has had a remarkable life. He was a missionary in the 1960s, but he left the mission field with the express purpose of becoming a millionaire. When he told me that I asked him, "Bobby, why the sudden change of direction from mission field to money?"

Bobby said, "I soon realized the great need of the mission field *was* money. So, I decided to return to the United States with the definite goal of being worth one million dollars within ten years. Of course, I had little business experience and no idea how to accomplish that goal."

I said, "That had to be an intimidating goal. A million dollars is a lot of money even today. In the 1960s it was quite a fortune. Did you make it?"

"Yes," he said, "I did. And then I lost it. But I made it back."

I remarked, "That had to be tough, to set such a high goal with no business experience and then make it, only to end up losing it all. How did you get your attitude up so you could try again after such a discouraging loss?"
He replied,

I got out my Bible and found all the verses where God promised provision, guidance, protection and blessing. I highlighted those verses in my Bible. Then I read those verses out loud to myself until my faith was strong enough to begin again.

Of course, my logic told me those verses would not help me, since the facts were the exact opposite of those promises. But Mark, when logic and common sense tell you that everything is over and you are never going to be anything but what you are, you have to push back against the natural with the supernatural.

"Christian gibberish. Ridiculous!" you say? Perhaps. I am merely passing it on without comment as a suggested method for gaining control over your emotions in tough times.
Does it work? Well, I will give you the rest of the story just as Mr. Dollar related it to me.

I was not young anymore and I was quite discouraged at times. I was praying and pondering how to recover from my mistakes, but I could see no way forward.

I was teaching a Sunday school class at the time, and during this period, a young man joined my group. His name was Cecil Day. Though I was older, we took an immediate liking to each other. He had an idea for starting an economy motel chain, and a little later, asked me to be in charge of franchising it.

I accepted on the spot and then drove to the public library to see if there were any books available on franchising a business. I knew nothing about the subject.

That motel chain was started and built with Mr. Dollar running the franchise end of the business. It was eventually sold for $250 million. I don't know how much of that Bobby received, but I think I have made my point.

The next time you drive past a Days Inn, remember that a man—an unqualified man at that—who spoke uplifting words out loud to himself to build his faith after failure—a man with no qualifications for what he was asking for, a man who overcame great discouragement—helped put that building on that spot. And hundreds of others just like it all over the world.

Incidentally, I use the same method as Mr. Dollar to get my faith back up when I'm down and will continue to until the day I pass from this life.

If you are of a different faith, then find the scriptures of your own faith that particularly encourage you. If you have no religious beliefs at all, then put the most compelling thoughts from your favorite authors in front of you and speak them out loud to yourself. Help yourself as you would help another. When the man in the mirror needs help, help him. Help him with your spoken words that strengthen the soul and defy defeat.

Also, cut off any negative influences, especially the news if you cannot watch it without being angered or discouraged. Our thoughts and feelings are greatly influenced by the most recent things we allow in. One of my favorite thoughts regarding not being disturbed by the corrupt affairs of this world goes something like this:

The times are dark.

Perhaps they are, but all I have to decide is what I am going to do with my own time here.

And that brings me to a related point. To turn down the voices of defeat and turn up the voice of faith is a fight *always*, not sometimes. The one person that we have the most conversations with and are influenced the most by is our own self. When I feel weak or discouraged, I must turn that internal conversation around with some self-talk like this:

> I have the faith for this. Things have a way of working out well for me and have many times in my life. It is going to get better. Years ago, I never thought I would get this far.

> If I don't know what to do, then I'll find or meet someone who does. I don't have to know everything. There is always someone who can meet this need. God can send the right person or provide a solution today. Besides, I can quit anytime, so why quit right now? I will just "push out from the edges" a little each day and keep chipping away at it.

And I should thank Dr. Mark Rutland for the idea of "push out from the edges," which I read in his *New York Times* bestselling book, *ReLaunch*. It's a great phrase to encourage us all: in order to keep moving forward, all we need to do is just "push out a little from the edges" a little each day.

I Practice What I Preach

I have lived what this book teaches. In fact, this very book itself is a perfect example of putting my own advice into practice.

When the unbidden and unwelcome thought was presented to my mind that I should write about how to use practical wisdom in all the major decisions of life, the very idea seemed ridiculous to the point of absurdity. It was entirely overwhelming.

I thought,

There are famous millionaires and billionaires and psychologists and preachers by the dozens writing books on money and life. They are the men and women qualified for that—not me. Who am I to take on such a task?

Besides, I'm not good at writing in an interesting style. And I detest writing! When I write something, it's as dry as Texas wind. The very thought of *me* attempting such a task and making it something interesting and of value to readers is ridiculous.

I am not exaggerating my doubts; if anything, they were worse than I am painting them. But I could not escape the feeling that it should be done—and that *I should do it*!

We all have thoughts that are whimsical and should be ignored, but when something is gnawing at you from the inside and keeps gnawing at you despite a sincere effort to ignore it, do not dismiss it just because it seems ridiculous or impossible.

An invitation from God to enlarge your life is identifiable by its uneasy persistence. If a thought eats at you and will not be dismissed over a considerable period of time, you might want to pay attention to it.

Then, if you decide it is something you are to do, do not make the mistake of trying to clear the ground ahead of you by human logic. Man was not given an intellect to rationalize obedience, but to execute plans; the best ones being Divinely inspired. Remember, anything God calls you to do will immediately seem impractical because He will never call you to do anything that you can do without Him.

As I write these lines, it is ten o'clock in the evening. I am tired, and my family is asleep. But I wanted to do something today that at least has the chance of making my future better.

I try to move toward something bigger for at least one hour every day.

Men and women who succeed do not jump from idea to idea. They focus on one thing. They apply all their efforts to one consuming intention. They don't have the answers either. What they do have is focus and darn near inexhaustible persistence.

I still do not know if this effort of mine in writing will bear fruit. In the early years, many questions tried to invade my thoughts constantly: Will a publisher ever even read it? How does one even find a publisher? Is what I have written any good? What exactly do I do to get a book published anyway? If a publisher ever looks at it, will it be printed? If so, will anyone buy it? I kept my head down and kept my focus on doing what I knew I *could do* that day.

As I write these words, I do not know the answer to many questions about what is ahead for this project. I simply decided to obey that persistent inner tug, and I began by trying to write a little bit every day.

Years have now passed, during which I have struggled with the task—sometimes, I admit, even setting it aside as more pressing concerns took over—and constantly pushing back against the doubts. I felt it should be done. I knew I was not the most qualified, but I was willing to try—and keep trying until it was done. That is where all success comes from.

I am well aware that the odds of a book written by an unknown person being accepted by a national publisher and then being widely read are just slightly more than the chance that it will be discovered that I am the rightful king of England. But I am not going to let the fears and doubts and odds against it keep me from attempting what is in my heart to do!

I wrote it down as a goal. I put some time into acting on it every day. And I will push until the work is completed or until I am guided into a more perfect direction. I will move forward, and I will persist. I will use self-talk, scriptures, and anything else that will help me to lean *into* my goal, instead of talking myself out of it.

In other words, I am putting into practice what I am telling you to do. When you have an idea that you think you should act on, *step toward it*, even when you do not have all the answers—or even know the right questions to ask. Do something to move toward it every day, and don't let the fear of the unknown or the inevitable discouragements decide your future.

If you try, failure *is* possible. But if you never even try, something less than you want for your life is a certainty. I just watched an interview with a billionaire. He said that he had expected to fail in most of the things he had ever attempted but knew that he would rather attempt them and fail than never try just so that he could avoid the risk of failure.

I felt like a fool and a failure when I began writing. After a full year and a half of working late into the night, trying to put coherent thoughts on paper, I deleted everything I had written—*everything*!

Forgive the bluntness, but it wasn't worth spit. I would not have paid one dime to read the whole lot of it, and I am not kidding. I cannot tell you how discouraged I felt.

Many times, I pushed forward while fighting the feeling that I had foolishly misjudged that "still small voice" within me—the one urging me into this seemingly unsuitable effort. At times so frustrated that I wrote while fighting back tears, I pushed myself to keep trying to find words that might make a difference to someone.

Then, disgusted with the results, after eighteen months I finally admitted my whole writing direction to date had been wrong—*and I started over*.

I have given this work an hour or two (or six) each day for a dozen years at the time I am writing these words. It has not come easily. Sometimes I labored for weeks over a few paragraphs and then deleted them all in disgust. On another occasion, I had worked on a complicated subject for months, was finally satisfied with the results, and then accidentally erased those months of labor and had to start over.

If one day you actually hold a published copy of one of my books in your hands and it is commercially successful, then you will be holding a critical lesson about building a better life for yourself:

When you have a passion for doing something or when you have an unbidden idea that keeps pulling at you for years, begin. There is no hope for better until one begins.

And don't let doubts, fears, setbacks, discouragements, or even failure itself stop you. Act on your ideas a little bit every day! Just do something every day. Nothing ventured, nothing gained. The having comes from the doing.

Even the Bible says not to "[despise] the day of small things [or beginnings]." (Zechariah 4:10, Amplified Bible) To state the obvious, you have to learn to ride a bike by attempting to ride one. Skinned knees are part of the deal. Success comes from persistently attempting to do what you don't yet know how to do.

There was a line from the original *Star Wars* movie I still remember. Han Solo is in a dire situation and Luke Skywalker asks him if he knows how impossible the odds of success are. Han Solo retorts, "Never tell me the odds, kid."

I feel that part of my reason for being here—for being given the gift of my life—is to encourage people to act on their ideas and to help them see that, if they handle their finances and private lives with moral restraint and common sense, the benefits far outweigh the sacrifices. In other words, I am here to share with others how to use:

Common Sense for a Prosperous Life

I am on a mission to put millions of mothers and fathers on the right track concerning how to handle life, marriage, and money so that their children have secure and loving homes to grow up in and examples lived out before them that are worth following.

A critic might say, "What a goal for a middle-aged, blue-collar contractor tucked away in obscurity repairing homes." My answer is, *I don't listen to that voice.* If you don't want to try, any excuse is good enough; and if you do—none are.

So, what excuse are you allowing to hold you back?

I have only this one life to live, and to the best of my ability I will not accept living any more of it being beaten down by the common-place life that was handed me, or my current limitations, or the long odds against getting out to a new level—*and neither should you.*

Except for those born as royalty, everybody starts out as a "nobody." So, if you have some idea that gnaws at you and will not go away, even if it seems beyond your current know-how, then begin. And we can all aid our movement forward by perfecting our work right where we are. Life is happening right now. Until bigger doors open, look for what you can do right where you are.

When I feel that my progress is too slow or too much in doubt, I ask myself, "What if *this* is as good as it gets?" I have found that for some curious reason instead of demoralizing me, this question boosts my conscious gratitude. It increases my satisfaction with my life, just as it is for now, and encourages me in my plans. I think it helps because it takes my mind off the gap between where I am and where I wish to be. You might try it.

A Most Unusual Event

Many years ago, when I was a much younger man, I was at church on a Sunday evening during the Easter season. I was sitting through the service doubtfully pondering if there even was a God. I certainly could see little evidence of it in my life at the time. As I looked at the props on stage that had been used in the Easter play, including the stage set with the painted Styrofoam stone rolled away from the opening of the empty tomb, I thought, "What a fantastic tale. I wonder if all this is true. You sure can't prove it from my life."

After all, if you consider the Christ story logically it is quite a bit to take in as fact. I was so discouraged that my logical doubts seemed quite reasonable. I was considering the subject dispassionately for a few minutes, and I concluded that the historical evidence that Jesus had actually existed was too overwhelming to dismiss, quite aside from any religious convictions. I also reflected on the words of Christ I had read in the Bible and concluded, not from any religious conviction but from logic, that no mere man could have spoken words so compelling while at the same time, be making up delusional tales. Nor could any group of people collude to formulate, and then record separately, such a remarkable story, and defend the story to the death.

I then considered the implications of the story, if it were true. If He died and rose from the grave what was the object of the exercise? Where did He go when He left the grave? Heaven can't be the right answer; He was already there before He left. Where did He want to go when He left that grave that He was not able to go before? *Where* did He go? *Where is He?*

I swear, it was as if I had never heard the story of Jesus or a single Christian sermon in my life. The thought came to me from pure logic: He left that grave so He could live in … *me!*

The story suddenly made logical sense. He wanted to live in me but couldn't. I was too unclean. He had to pay the price to clean me up. He died in my place then left the tomb—to come live inside me!

The next thought that occurred to me was,

If the God who created the universe is in me, then what difference does it make how I feel or what I ask for, *there are no limits.*

I am not just going to pray for my discouragement to cease or my life to improve. I am going to ask for what I would really want if there were no limits at all placed on my requests.

If God created everything, then He can certainly handle whatever I ask for, no matter how big it seems to me.

I was sick of struggling through a meaningless life—at least one that had little meaning to me. Now, if you suddenly realized you weren't just praying to air, but, in your heart, truly standing before God himself, and He leaned forward and kindly asked what He could do for you, what would you ask for?

I asked for five things. I had never thought of them before. The thoughts and the requests were completely spontaneous, but I meant every word. Here are the five things I asked for. See what you think of my requests.

I said,

I am sick and tired of doing nothing more than repairing homes and struggling to pay bills. Give me this:

1. I want something to do that is worth my life.
2. I want to love it so much I would do it for free.
3. I want to be the best in the world at it.
4. And I want it to produce wealth, for my own family and many others.

Then I added one more thing:

5. Lord, I am so emotionally exhausted that even if you gave it all to me, I am too burned out emotionally to do anything about it. I need the spirit that was on the biblical warrior Caleb when he went through the wilderness for forty

years, and then, still youthful in strength, con-
quered the choicest mountain in the Promised
Land. I know I am asking for a mountain, but
if You are God, then ... *Give me this mountain!*

My deeply inward thoughts of the last few minutes had
kept me unaware of the service going on around me. I just kept
whispering over and over to God under my breath, "Give me
this mountain! Give me this mountain!" I must have muttered
that prayer to myself twenty times. I felt a depth of need only
the truly desperate know. Believing myself to be so far from
anything that felt like a rewarding life ... discouraged nearly
beyond continuing for fear nothing would ever change ...
and for so long lost as to what to do about it ... I prayed as
if I were praying for my very life, which I was.

Then, as I was whispering my prayer to God—"Give me
this mountain"—over and over, the pastor suddenly stopped
his sermon in the two-thousand-seat church and said,

"I have just heard in my heart a word from the Lord for
someone here. The Lord says this to you: "'I have heard
your prayer, and I give you this mountain! I also give
you the spirit of Caleb who grew mightier as he aged. I
empower you to do the unusual for My name's sake and
for My glory. Yes, *I give you this mountain!*'"

My head snapped up toward the podium. I was stunned.
My mouth literally fell open in shock. God was using a man's
mouth to answer me in an audible voice. And if you chalk
that one up to coincidence, then you are willfully blind. I had
received an audible answer from God.

Many years later I shared this incident with my sister. She
remarked, "That's an amazing story, but that was many years
ago. Do you still believe it was for you? Do you really think
it will happen? Why do you think it's taking so long?"

I answered her the best I could this way:

Sis, if I had only asked for something to do that was worth my life and that I loved doing, He could have brought it to me the next day. Within a few years, He could have also made me the best in the world at it.

But I also asked for wealth and a great deal of it. And I think that's the issue. There is real risk in answering that one. A lot of money can be a dangerous thing for a parent to give a child, even as an adult. Whatever He has in mind, I think He wants to prepare me so that my relationship with Him is not harmed by it and my success is handled with maturity and discretion.

It can be a dangerous thing to give someone success and wealth. Look to Hollywood or the tabloids for endless examples of just how harmful it can be.

I still fully expect every word of what God promised, but now I have enough sense to trust Him for the timing, too. It's better to wait sometimes and let God decide when. I had rather go up at the right time than to go up too soon and come back down in an embarrassing crash.

I told my sister, "I know it is going to happen. I think it will be through the books that I am writing. And I trust that these years of waiting are an important part of getting it right."

When I prayed that prayer so many years ago, what I desperately wanted was a life that fulfilled me and relieved me of financial or business worries. We all want that. But time has reshaped me, and now, an important part of God's response is when He said, "for My Name's sake." Those many years ago, that was probably a minor note to me.

In Matthew 9:17, Jesus said new wine must be poured into new wineskins, because if new wine were poured into old wineskins, the skins would expand too quickly and not be strong enough to safely hold the reaction to the new wine.

I choose to believe that our prayers are always heard, and answered, but in more perfect ways than we can pray them. And I say that even though I myself still wait.

I believe my Common Sense for a Prosperous Life books will sell. And when they sell in big numbers my life will be changed, but so will the lives of many others. I hope that those who read them will realize that just because they may feel inadequate or discouraged, just because they are out of hope, despite their current reality, there is a higher reality above our sight that is wise, merciful and not subject to our current limitations. Even before this day is out, one phone call or event can open to you a future where everything looks different.

It is my dream that after reading my books families will be strengthened. Men will be committed to being better fathers and husbands, and women to being better mothers, wives and professionals. And yes, businesses will be birthed, and future men and women of wealth created from currently humble circumstances. That can happen to me and you. Why do I say so? Because a flash of inspired thought is the most powerful force on earth. Mine and yours just as much as anyone else's.

And, if you are reading this, whether this book was just published or it is decades old and I am long past, He had *you* in mind, too. He had this book find its way to you for a reason.

There was not much to me as a man and absolutely nothing left in my tank when I had that dramatic prayer encounter. That man was too small and too defeated to hold much. But little can become much when God is in it, given a few years. If you want a bigger life, you must be willing to be reshaped into a man or woman who can handle it, and that takes time.

Answered prayers for a life-mate, money, favorable events, restored relationships, and promotions—all these can come, and in truth do come every day to people, probably millions of times a month worldwide. But to remake what we are on the inside is like turning an aircraft carrier. It takes time and a lot of ocean to turn that big ship. Just so, preparing us for what we want may require a few years of waiting, frustration, disappointments and discouragement. That is not bad news. It can actually serve us. In a battle, it's the man with scars that knows what he is doing.

So here is a key: hard times and dry seasons, with apparently nothing going right, have permanent value that will only become clear to you later. God is careless about nothing when it comes to answering our prayers. He said, "Ask, and it shall be given." (Matthew 7:7, KJV) And if in our immaturity we ask amiss? Then He is wise enough to give us the equivalent good.

God is the Great Alchemist. He turns our battles and our losses to our advantage. But that does not mean we are quickly "all better." It does mean that all of it will be used as fuel in our future if we don't give up on our own life. No matter the loss or lack, and despite the bleakness we all can't help but feel at times, the way forward is still there and will open at the right time. Don't give feelings, facts, and appearances the final word over your life. Stay true to your request that your life amount to more than is around you now. It may just be that it is coming by a different route than expected. You must survive the bad times to get to the good ones. Be sure you stay around for the best part of your journey.

One Talent, One Idea Is Enough

Every successful man or woman you meet has had the same battles as you and I may be having now. They heard the same voice whisper to them that they were going to stay where they were, that they would never escape, never become someone larger, never achieve their dreams—in a word, that they were never going to have what the better life they wanted. Everyone has heard that voice. The leaders in every walk of life around you heard it, but they found a way to keep going in spite of it. So must you and me.

What I am about to say is not specific to my Christian faith even though it comes from the Bible. Any of you who believe differently can easily apply it. It is recorded (Matthew 25:14-30, Luke 19:11-27) that Jesus told a parable about a servant who, having only one talent, discounted his abilities as too meager and refused to use his only gift. He was severely rebuked for being lazy and irresponsible with that which he had been given.

The point is this: one talent *is* enough. If one talent is all we have then one talent is all we need. And it may be a talent we do not even know yet that we possess. After all, the thought of writing had never crossed my mind before I was led to do it. We shall yet see what comes of it, for others and myself. Faith is *action* in the face of an unknown outcome.

Some people are so loaded with gifts that they overwhelm us. They can speak, write, sing, dance, and inspire. Others, rich with different gifts, build business empires. But there are those—like me with these books I write—whose entire life after many years of anonymous preparation was intended to hit one major note perfectly.

How many talents we were given is up to God. If you only have one skill, that one thing is all God needs to completely change your future—if you will use it.

For years I was discouraged because I thought I had no business talent at all and never would get beyond driving a police car. Though I loved being of service to others in that capacity, I wanted more for myself and my family than those skills could provide. Later in life, the same thoughts crept in again, as decades ticked by while I was over-working as a home improvement contractor. These are both honorable trades, but for some reason they did not fulfill me. I still needed more. When the idea of writing intruded upon my mind, I thought it sheer folly. I could not have been more dismissive toward it if I had been asked to become an astronaut.

I did not know this then, but I am proof of it now:

**_The fact that you know of no way for your
life to change means absolutely nothing._**

We get in life what we are willing to accept as final. All "talents" appear after a decision is made to find them and use them. Like I have said, treasures don't lay on the surface.

I was a B-average high school graduate who became a policeman who became a roofer. You could not make up a more pedestrian life. And I could see no way out of it. I never had the remotest notion of what I could do to change it—not until an idea popped into my head during an unimportant conversation. The idea was that _I_ should write a book to help people make important decisions with greater common sense and clarity for the welfare of their family.

Eventually, that seemingly errant thought that appeared unbidden during a casual conversation changed my focus. Let me ask you, can you really swallow the lie that at the right time a single inspired thought cannot unexpectedly drop into your mind and unchain your brain? _Give me a break!_

As I said, I had no idea I should—or could—write. The barest thought of it had never crossed my mind in any form. So here is another life lesson learned: if you keep feeling the urge to "get on the bus," then God has already put the price for the ride in your pocket—or in the pocket of someone you will meet on your way to the bus stop.

**_Don't keep checking your pockets.
GO GET ON THE BUS!_**

Just one thought, one unanticipated event, one casual comment or suggestion, one undiscovered talent, one chance meeting or one kingdom connection, can redirect your life.

I once attended an inspirational talk given by Rocky Bleier of the famed 1970s Pittsburgh Steelers football team. Some consider this the greatest team ever assembled in the history of the National Football League.

During his presentation, Rocky said something that encouraged me greatly and makes my point well. He said that he was too short and too slow to play football as a running back, so he quit the Steelers. But a friend called him and said, "Don't fire yourself, Rocky. You may get fired, but come back and make *them* fire you."

He took his friend's advice and returned, fully expecting to be cut from the team. But the coach had noticed that Rocky was a great blocker, a skill that Rocky had never thought about as his position was running back. But that one talent at blocking was enough to win him a place on the roster—and four Super Bowl rings as a member of one of the greatest sports dynasties in history!

When you are down, just remind yourself, "All I need is one talent to succeed. And it does not have to be a talent I am even aware of yet. One talent was enough for four Super Bowl rings!"

Prayer Takes Us Further, Faster

There is always the possibility that unexpected events can turn our plans upside down. But we should also consider that it is just as possible that unexpected events can accelerate our plans. When we feel stuck or perplexed, we should ask for help.

No matter what it looks like now, life can improve, and often, helpful events take us further, faster than we thought possible. Throughout human history men and women of every nation and faith have asked for aid and guidance in prayer—and received it.

Even while typing these words, I remember how difficult my wife and I expected it to be to provide our three daughters with college educations and solid, reliable cars when it was time for those expenses. In hindsight, providing the tuition and cars, all paid for, was much easier than we had thought possible, done easily and at just the right time.

It is statistically provable that men and women who pray live longer, healthier, happier lives. Surely, no matter our differing personal beliefs, each of us can humble ourselves and ask our Higher Power for help in our own way. Prayer is simply asking for help, offering thanks in anticipation of the answer, and grateful acknowledgement of the supply when received. We can all do that, no matter how uncertain we feel when we do it.

I have asked for help and guidance many times, for personal problems and in business: the global economic meltdown from 2007 to 2011, looming financial threats, family issues, and years of uncertainty that felt more like a grind than really living. The voices that so easily come to us all still come to me, too: "How many more years will you repair houses? What if this is all your life will ever amount to?"

So yes, I still have to resist the same thoughts you may have when you ponder your own future. I still repair houses for my daily bread, making life-changing contributions to very few beyond my family. But let me say this: Once you see what you think to be the best direction to take, faith means you take the first step, even though you cannot see past it, and unless you realize you have made a mistake, you continue even when you feel inadequate. Faith is not a feeling; it is a life you learn to live.

I was always willing to pray for help, and then do two simple things: go to work and keep going.

Whether Christian, a member of another faith, atheist, or agnostic your best shot is always to follow your heart, even if it means going against the odds. That Inner Voice will lead you unerringly. And, yes, even when you are on the right track, the path will include periods of deep discouragement. Those feelings are a part of the process of getting *anything* worthwhile done.

I am mature enough now to know that these feelings of inadequacy are just a normal part of life. They have been an unavoidable part of my success story and will be a part of yours. Discouragements and detours and delays and apparent dead-ends will have their shot at you. Your job is to find a way through them. It is the dream inside you that will make the way if you hang onto it when the path is dark and heaven silent. You can't go wrong asking for help in prayer, and despite what you feel and see just assume you were heard.

Today, I can do a little more toward my goal. I may feel tired or discouraged, yes, I may need a day off now and then, but I can and will do a little something *today*. And one day, in my dream of having an influence for good far beyond my life as it is now, I will be somewhere and look around me in a moment of unexpected discovery and realize, *This is it! I am standing in it!*

One of my favorite people in American history is botanist and scientist George Washington Carver. Mr. Carver recorded these comments about this very subject.

> "As I worked on projects which fulfilled a real human need forces were working through me which amazed me. I would often go to sleep with an apparently insoluble problem. When I woke the answer was there. Why, then, should we who believe in God be so surprised at what God can do with a willing man ..."

There are two key points here: no one is smart enough alone, so ask for the help; and, we don't need to have the solutions to start. No one is likely to step toward their dreams if they weigh their mind down with all that mess. Once you have an idea that will not leave you alone, breathe life into it by taking small steps toward it—*and refuse to think too far ahead.*

Our biggest enemy is the nitpicking human tendency to try to have the answer for everything, but we will never take the first step if we think that way. Just "get on the bus" and do whatever you can think of to do today. That makes it manageable. Like the Nike sportswear slogan says: "Just do it!"

A close friend who was very successful commented on the outrageous odds against my books ever selling. He then asked why I would spend many years and many dollars on the project. He was not trying to discourage me; he was just curious. I explained it to him this way:

The idea to do this was not mine. It was brought to me, and it refused to leave my mind over a matter of years.

Personally, I was opposed to the very thought. I knew the long odds and the years of work it would take. But it came down to deciding to trust that inner voice within. And as much as I did not want to do it—as it certainly seemed like dry work to me at the time—I did not want to live and die where I was. I wanted to take my shot at the success America offers those who dream and dare and do.

You and I both know that these intuitive feelings are not based on human logic. It is our only faculty that originates from outside us, and we both have followed it at times in our businesses with good results. So the long odds can't be the standard when I am acting in response to a persistent intuitive lead.

I know the odds are greatly against any unknown person selling books on any subject in any great number. I choose to believe that I will be the exception. Otherwise, why try? Why claim I want something more and then refuse to act because the odds are long? What difference does that make? The odds are zero if I don't try.

I'm taking my shot at a better life.

He said, "Yep, that's what I did."

I have been through the waiting years when my mind told me, "The average life is all there will ever be for you, Mark. You just don't have what others do."

I have been through the working years when the same voice switched to, "You don't have what it takes to do this. You don't have the skills. There are too many hurdles. It is obvious to everyone how insecure and out of place you are."

Liars, both ... *unless you listen to them.*

Pray for guidance and when even a small opportunity that seems good for you is presented be willing to step toward it. Vigilance, prayer, and a willingness to stretch will take you further, faster.

In the meantime, make good use of the time at hand. Take care of your job, get your finances in order, and work on the things in your private life that need correcting. Do not be impetuous or rash, just have your eyes and ears open. We are never as far from positive events as it feels like to us. A great deal can change with one idea, one phone call, and in a short period of time. Appreciate the good things that are in the rhythm of your life as it is. There is no need to rev your motors to the breaking point before you have a race to run.

In the next chapter, we'll look at some practical, helpful habits you can develop to help move your life forward. Then, in chapter five, we will discuss how to unchain your brain to *create* the way to your desire.

CHAPTER 4
WISDOM NUGGETS

If you wish to rise in influence and income, it is important that you choose well the information that will influence your thoughts. Many of us, including myself, were born with a tendency to lean toward the negative in our thoughts. I have found it necessary to shut off the daily news and any reading that tends to produce negative thoughts and feelings. As they say, "No thought lives in your head rent-free."

We should not be preoccupied with events over which we have little to no control, especially when it is easy to become emotionally invested in them. I recently had an instructive personal example along these lines.

A friend of mine is a recent immigrant to the United States. He sees America through a fresh lens, rather than with the view of someone who grew up here and is accustomed to the living standards. He picked me up at the airport not long ago, and, during the ride home, I made a negative comment about how current political trends would harm our economy. I also registered a complaint about the Atlanta traffic we were stuck in.

He remarked,

Mark, when I look at this traffic, I see two things: first, here almost everyone who chooses to work can afford their own car. And second, I see an economy that puts so many people to work that traffic gridlock is normal in every city in your nation. And even though government over-regulation and debt will hamper prosperity and freedom, there is real opportunity here.

I have traveled the world. There is no other country with individual freedom and opportunity like this anywhere, not even close. You are seeing and thinking upside down. As a man of business, I suggest you consider what these thoughts can cost you.

There is wealth and opportunity here like nowhere else on earth, and the traffic you are complaining about is actually the proof of it. Mark, if you can supply just one need for the driver of each car we pass on just this one trip, you can retire. You are riding through the greatest opportunity that has ever existed for anyone willing to think and create and work. Anyone who believes otherwise is blind to the point of absurdity.

Do you see how powerfully our thoughts can affect our chances for success? Two people can be in the same place looking at the same thing, and just because of how they process the information, one can be putting up mental barriers to success while the other is more confident by the day.

So, this is key:

Any person or activity or line of thought that drains energy or optimism from you is to be avoided. If it is hindering you, then avoid it or get rid of it altogether.

It is not your job to fix the world; it is your job to fix *your* world.

The actions of a government, a political party, or any other third party, no matter who they are, will never change your life one percent as much as your own choices will.

When I wake up, I spend a few minutes reading scriptures that strengthen my faith. When I am driving, seventy percent of the time I am listening to an encouraging recording. My wife and I put something into our spirits every day to strengthen our belief that, despite the problems of the world, being here is a blessing and we were put here to make a positive contribution.

In addition to cutting off all negative influences, here are five more practical things you can do to elevate your life's trajectory.

1. Read to a Purpose

I remember an occasion when my daughter Scarlett and I were talking in our home's library. She looked around and asked me, "Dad, have you read all these books?"

"Yes, almost all of them," I said.

She asked, "Why? Why did you read all these books? What are they about?"

I answered her this way:

Well, first of all, I have never met a very successful man or woman that did not read. Not one. Since I did not like reading, but also did not want to stay a policeman all my life, I had to force myself to read every day until it became a habit. That took a long time, but it was worth it.

Scarlett, the biggest challenge any of us have when it comes to building a good life is within our own mind—in the way we think. Most of us, by our nature, are quick to think negatively. Instead of deciding what we want to do, we think of all the problems and obstacles. And truthfully, not many of us are exceptionally gifted. I'm not. Only a few exceptionally gifted men and women are born, and, of course, they rise in the world to become household names in sports or entertainment or business.

But, unless you are born with a mind or body that is wired in some exceptional way, you will have to grow in the way you think if you want to earn your share of happiness and material comforts in this world.

To do that, you will need to learn how the men and women who do succeed think, and reading their books can help a lot.

In fact, believe it or not, reading their books is even better than knowing the people personally. In the book, the author has distilled his or her best thoughts into writing. The book can travel with you anywhere you go. The book never gets tired of teaching whenever you want to learn and always is ready with only the best thoughts. It is as if the author is always ready to talk to you from his or her heart, whenever you are in the mood to listen. A book never gets irritable with your mistakes and never gets too tired to help. A person can't do that.

It may seem a privilege if you can say, "Oh, I am friends with that great man or woman," but, in truth, you will get a hundred times more that matters if you will buy their book and read it. And that would still be the best use of your time even if you did know them personally.

After a moment of thought, I added,

Starting years ago, if I happened to cross paths with a happy and successful man or woman, I would ask them which books they considered the most important to their success. It was just common sense to me that that would be a lot more helpful than browsing for books on my own.

Over a period of a few years, I began to see from the books they recommended what was important to men and women who were a lot smarter and a lot more successful than I was.

You see, Scarlett, general knowledge is worthless. Anyone who is smart about a lot of subjects can be replaced for a few hundred dollars—the cost of a set of encyclopedias. [This conversation took place in the beginning of our now abundantly available Internet resources.] Scarlett, I have a friend who reads three or four hours a day. He can talk about a great number of subjects intelligently and in amazing detail, but all his reading has not made his life any better. In fact, as bright as he is, he has trouble making his house payment because he reads nothing to any practical purpose. He just expands his ego with more and more meaningless knowledge.

But I wanted to make a more capable man out of myself. As a young policeman, I knew nothing about business or money, or even how to be a good husband and father. My dad left before I was born and my mom worked a lot. But no matter how we begin, it is the responsibility of every man and woman to learn how to provide a secure, loving home for living and thriving in. That's what we all want. But, statistically, these things rarely happen when we leave them to chance. I suppose most people just assume that they will know what to do when the time comes—but I didn't want to do that. There just wasn't much to me, and I knew I would need help.

About the time that I was becoming an adult I met a very successful man. I told him I wanted to make something out of myself. He was kind enough to tell me that he started out just like many others, with no father in the home and no clear direction, but that our future could be changed by the books we read and the people we associate with, and I believed him. That comment changed my life.

I waved my arm at the full shelves in the room.

These books helped me change who I was inside, which of course, slowly changed my life over time. Still, I would not recommend that you read this many books. I now think it is better to pick only a few books—twenty or fewer for a lifetime—and read and reread them until your life is a living example of the principles they teach.

Reading only a few of the very best books ever written over and over is, I think, more effective than continuously reading different books, even good ones.

To be honest with you, honey, I have not grown as much as I would have hoped. Even so, due to my self-education from these books, my life has far surpassed what it would have been by birth and chance. And that is only because forty years ago I decided to become someone larger than who I was.

Unless you are one of those fortunate people born with a definite passion to pursue some particular line, you will have to *decide* to make something out of yourself. And I am not just talking about earning money. Almost all the circumstances of your life are eventually determined by how you think and the choices you make.

Most people's choices make their life much harder than it has to be. They want to play now and pay later. But that can turn out to be a very expensive choice. It is far better to pay now for what you want and play later, particularly once you reach adulthood. Of course, everyone needs to be young and a teenager and enjoy those years. Do you understand these things?

"Yes, Dad," she said.
"Then does that answer your question?"
"Yes, but it sounds like being a grown-up is kind of hard."
I gave that a bit of thought, then answered,

Well, I guess it is at times. But we can make it easier if we are willing to do the work, which is exactly what I am talking to you about.

Most people try to avoid doing the things that need to be done because they don't want to do them. They don't want to do the hard things; they want to have fun instead.

That is normal, but I think it proves to be a poor choice in the long run. You should pay the price for what you want instead of waiting for someone else to give it to you. In a free country you are supposed to come to your own aid and make yourself valuable to society and be rewarded for it. In a country like America, you are never helpless, unless you choose to be. And you can help yourself a lot if you read carefully chosen books. Do you understand?

"Yes, I do," she said.

2. Do the Hard Things First

Continuing the conversation, I said,

I remember a television commercial that made this point well. There is a company called Fram that makes oil filters for cars. They are very good filters, so they are more expensive than those of their competitors.

A few years ago, they ran a commercial which showed two men, one a car repairman working on an engine and the other a man who sold auto parts. The second man said, "Fram oil filters: Pay me now …" and the auto repairman then said, "… or pay me later."

What they were saying was that you could either spend what it took to buy the right filter or cut corners and pay for it when your car broke down from cheap filters and dirty oil. But one way or the other, you were going to pay. It was a great commercial and a great lesson for real life.

Because life says, "You can pay for what you want now and enjoy the benefits after the work is done or play now and pay for your choice later—*but pay you will.*"

Most people avoid doing anything that requires real effort unless they have to. They choose instead to take the easy way. But, if you try always to take the easy path, those choices have consequences and life is going to get harder and harder later on.

So, it is best to do the work first and get it out of the way.

You don't *have* to choose to live that way, but you are going to pay life's bill one way or the other because there *is* a price for every choice—even the choice to take what appears to be the easy way. Do you know what I mean?

"Yes, I do," she said. Then she asked, "But everyone can't succeed, can they?"

3. Don't Let Other People Become Your Reference Point

This was an important lesson, too, so I replied,

> If you mean become rich, no. But becoming a competent and independent man or woman and becoming rich are two different things. I think anyone with a healthy mind can make choices that will lead to a satisfying life, but I do not think becoming rich is a choice we can directly control.

> It is true that wealth is usually the result of personal initiative and effort, but it also requires a fortunate combination of events not completely subject to our control. Because there are so many things in each life which none of us control, it is pointless to compare your life with anyone else's—and that is especially true regarding money. The only thing that usually comes from that is discouragement or pride.

> My advice is to resist the temptation to compare your life with anyone else's. Those are easy words to say but very hard to do. Comparing ourselves to others is a reflexive instinct. However, it is always the wrong thing to do.

> Out of the hundreds of events that took that person to where they are, you probably don't have five major turning points in common with them, even though they may be in your same line of work and about your age.

> And you have no time to waste envying what is going on in someone else's life. An adult coveting someone else's life is no different from a spoiled child crying to play with another child's toys.

Our own life can become full and satisfying, but only after we embrace it.

Scarlett asked, "What does that mean? How do we do that?"

I thought about it and replied,

When a racehorse is not running as well as it should, the trainer will sometimes cover its eyes with something called "blinders." These keep the horse focused on the track ahead of it by removing its ability to see the other horses running beside it.

And it is remarkable how often an average running horse has blinders put on it and then begins to run his own race and becomes a standout winner.

Your job is to work your way through any undesirable circumstances *you* are in and begin to move toward whatever is important to you. So, you set your own goals, then put on blinders—just like they put on racehorses—so you can run your own race and ignore what is going on with anybody else. They have their own paths to walk out just as you do.

We all tend to think other people have it better than we do. The truth is, if everyone put their problems in a big hat and then drew out again at random, we would pay money to have our own lives back.

Finally, I looked at the library full of books again and said,

Even if you don't choose to go into business, no one can afford to be ignorant about money and life. The penalties are just too severe. These books taught me much about these things, and now you know why I have read them and why I hope one day you will read some of them, too.

When our daughters were young and maturing, we often talked about important life issues with all of them.

4. Be Smart About the Right Things

Since the length of a human life is limited, it is important to decide which things you will be smart about. It is not likely that knowing every negative news event going on in the world or being able to impress friends with your knowledge of sports trivia is going to help.

I'd recommend instead a healthy level of ambition, cultivating an agreeable personality, saving some money, taking personal responsibility for your own life, and using a good bit of common sense. Become smarter about those things, because those are the things allow you to secure your share of this world's happiness and comforts.

If you are deficient in these skills—and willing to remain that way—then your life is going to be harder than it has to be, and deservedly so. All five books in the *Common Sense for a Prosperous Life* series shed light on our most common blind spots.

You and I do not have to remain the way we are. We can decide to become larger. Men and women, like rubber bands, were made to be stretched.

Every line of thought either hinders or helps. And it's okay to just disregard some things, true or not. If it doesn't help you in some way, get rid of it. Negative things going on around you that you can't do anything about amount to nothing but weights that will slow you down. If you can't change it, then don't let it rob you of your daily happiness and future. I know bad things go on in this world, but I don't have to keep uploading them into my mind.

Be like a ship: it is surrounded by water, but it does not let any of it in. That way it gets to its desired destination. Keep your mind off-limits to problems or people that are nothing but a distraction and a hindrance.

And be smart about this: you don't need thirty years to change. Just a year is more than enough time to make huge steps forward. More change can happen in a few years than people imagine. Five years from today, your life could be so improved as to be unrecognizable to you now.

We don't have to remain who we are, what we are, or where we are. Get away from things that don't help and never can help and get smarter about the things that can. The five books in my *Common Sense for a Prosperous Life* series are a great place to start.

Make up your mind that in five years your life is going to be very different; and I don't care what your circumstances are right now.

The score at halftime is the most meaningless statistic in the world.

5. Use Each Day to a Purpose

The late Harvey Firestone, founder of the great Firestone Tire and Rubber Company, was dissatisfied with his effectiveness. He hired an expert in organization and asked the man to watch him closely over a period of time and then make any suggestions he thought appropriate. Mr. Firestone hired him with the understanding that he would be paid what Mr. Firestone thought appropriate for any improvements in efficiency resulting from the man's counsel. In other words, the man had to take the job on faith and prove his value to the great industrialist.

After watching Mr. Firestone closely over a period of weeks, the efficiency expert had only one suggestion—which Mr. Firestone implemented—and, after evaluating its worth,

Mr. Firestone sent the man a check for $25,000. That may not sound spectacular now, but, at the time, it was a fortune.

What suggestion accomplished so much for Harvey Firestone that he paid a fortune for it, even though he had no obligation binding him to such a fantastic sum? To a man already incredibly efficient with his time, what secret was worth paying several years' average wages for?

The man suggested Mr. Firestone take a 3" x 5" card and write down what he intended to accomplish the next day in the order it was to be done. That was it.

Now, if a man already organized enough to build an industrial empire found it that profitable a suggestion, what transformation could you and I produce in our own lives if we followed that program for five years—each day making something on the list a one hour investment to change our future?

For years I have used a 3" x 5" card to control my time. Here is today's card, which I wrote out last night before retiring. I will spell it out for you here, but on my cards I have developed a system of symbols that shortens the writing.

Up by 6:30 a.m.
Shower
Have breakfast; take vitamins
Scripture, mediate goals, prayer, gratitude: 30 minutes
Go to office
Upon returning home: exercise
Take care of any paperwork or phone calls from home office
Have dinner—no sweets after dinner!
Spend one to two hours working on books
7 p.m.—relax with the family
9 p.m.—retire; read something uplifting
Lights out at 10 p.m.

Almost every night, and for many years now, I have written instructions to myself for the next day on an index card. As you can see, I use this method to keep an organized schedule that addresses my spiritual, physical, and financial health. At least one activity must be an investment to increase my future income beyond my job, which, in this case, is spending at least one hour writing the words you are reading now.

I know some of you may be thinking, "If I had the leisurely schedule this guy has, I could do that, too, but it won't work with my schedule." And you may be right. Certainly, if you feel that way, it is not going to be something you sincerely apply.

But I will tell you this, for the first sixteen years I was building my home improvement business, the schedule I kept was just as demanding as that of a medical student when he or she interns, and I still used my cards to keep me on track. Of course, I did not have to write down anything about doing something to increase my future income because, once I went to work for myself, I was doing exactly that all day, every day.

Your tomorrows are determined by what you do *today*, and you have to create a long repeating pattern of productive days to change the trajectory of your life. As my dear friend, the late Leslie Hale put it, "Your future is following you." What he meant is that the seeds for your tomorrow were sowed yesterday. Your future is set by the consistent actions you sowed in your past. Consistent self-preparation and doing all you do—even the little things—in an excellent manner, all set future events in motion.

That's good news. It means we do have a good bit of control when we decide to use it. No matter how busy you are you can make a note to do at least one thing each day that has the

> *Don't judge each day by the harvest you reap but by the seeds that you plant.*
> —Robert Louis Stevenson

potential to lead you to a better life and a greater income in the future, and reading a book well suited to the purpose for fifteen minutes before retiring should be a part of that discipline.

Time is elusive, and unless it is captured and put to purposeful ends, it slips away, accomplishing little more than the maintenance of the existing routine. I rarely, if ever, put off doing anything, and almost every day I do something to help me create a more prosperous future that goes beyond the routine.

Even so, it is amazing how soon I get careless with my time if I go a few days without my schedule written out ahead on a 3" x 5" card. This simple system of having a written plan for how I will spend my time every day helps me to use it in a disciplined manner and invest it in activities that will make a difference. A man or woman is worth only as much as the things that they busy themselves with.

Human life is brief. Your opportunity to act is limited. There is a quote I read, attributed to the Buddha, which captures this point well: "The trouble is, we think we have time."

So get in the game. Get into the habit of doing something every day that plants a seed in your future. Before you retire each evening, or first thing in the morning, write down on a 3" x 5" card what you intend to do with the day, in the order you intend to do it, and be sure that some of it goes beyond the orderly maintenance of the life you already have.

In other words, some of your time should be used *every day* to take a step toward creating a more prosperous future. Get into the habit of *acting* instead of just thinking about it.

Small steps taken every day will amount to much over time. One hour per day is 365 hours in a year. That is the equivalent of forty-five days of work at eight hours a day! That is nine weeks per year devoted exclusively to improving your chances for larger responsibilities and income. In ten years, that small, consistent effort is almost *two solid years* of investment in your future—and that has to bear fruit eventually.

In every field of profitable activity worldwide there is an ongoing, earnest search for men and women who have something significant to contribute. Become one, and you won't have to worry about finding your place. The right door will open to your touch.

If your goal does not affect how you spend at least an hour of your time every day, then you don't have a goal.

Here is my most useful statement to you on time management: If you want a better future, make every day pay you something tomorrow.

Three accurate indicators that a man or woman has what it takes to succeed are:

1. They finish what they start.
2. They do not tolerate disorder around them. The condition of their home, yard, and cars reflect this.
3. They are decisive and mentally focused. They do not jump from one idea to another. They refuse to waste time.

You've now been given five very practical self-helps to move you higher, which you are already doing by reading this book:

1. Read to a Purpose
2. Do the Hard Things First
3. Don't Compare. Put on Blinders Concerning Other People
4. Be Smart About Things that Matter to Your Future
5. Use One Hour Each Day to Improve Your Future

Success is not the result of scattered activity. It is the result of plowing one deep furrow in a straight line. But what is your goal? The rest of *Unchain Your Brain* will help you move toward a series of deliberate objectives.

CHAPTER 5

WHEN THE *WHY* IS STRONG, THE *HOW* WILL COME

cannot tell anyone, not even my children, what they would succeed at. Usually, we are unsure on this point ourselves. But I can share with you the one common thread that all who succeed use to answer that question for themself. Something more than a non-specific desire to "do better" is needed, and in this chapter, I will describe what that something is. What you read in the remainder of this book is as reliable as a math equation and has produced positive and dramatic transformations in every person's life that used this open secret throughout all human history.

In the classic American movie, *Gone with the Wind*, the main character, Scarlett O'Hara, and her family, are starving among the ruins of their former estate in the post–Civil War South. An iconic scene features Scarlett walking through her war-torn property when, suddenly, this former daughter of wealth finds a single vegetable in the ground. In desperate hunger, she attempts to devour it, dirt and all. She chokes and then collapses, overcome with despair and defeat.

She has been taken from the heights of prewar privilege to destitute starvation. There is nothing ahead for her and her family but hunger and humiliation. The facts are bleak, and the changes that the war brought upon their former way of life are absolutely final.

Then something mysterious happens *inside of her* that will change every circumstance *outside of her*. She rises from the ground, stretches clenched fists toward heaven, and with everything in her soul defiantly declares, "As God is my witness, as God is my witness, they're not going to lick me. I'm going to live through this, and when it's all over, I'll never be hungry again. No, nor any of my folk!"

Reader, mark this well: an emotional need that sweeps all obstacles and objections aside as "irrelevant" is the only certain way for you and me to produce dramatic changes in our lives.

But how do we get there if the events of our lives do not put us into that intensely emotionalized state? The truthful answer is that I am not sure it is possible to intentionally produce that level of intensity. However, something only approximating it will serve our purpose, and that we can do.

Using a couple of examples, only slightly modified from real-life persons with which I am familiar, let's first note how an emotionalized thought, one crystal clear intention, can alter outcomes despite the most limiting of conditions.

Example 1

A father, after losing his very normal job, becomes increasingly humiliated by the necessities his family is deprived of. He feels an indignation building up within him that is more compelling than anything he has ever felt before. After snapping out of his depression, he arrives at a decision from which there is no retreat: "My wife and children will *not* live like this any longer, and neither will I! *I will not accept this.*"

Everything that had stopped him before from going out on his own, the need to hold onto his job ... the long odds against success ... his lack of education ... his lack of money ... the glaring fact that at this moment he has absolutely no idea what to do to make things better—all of these combined *could not be less important to him now.*

Before, when he had a regular income, whenever he thought about going into business on his own any one of those things seemed insurmountable. But now, he measures the whole lot of them with scornful disdain. To him, they are not so much as "the small dust of the balance." He has become *obsessed with improving his financial conditions!*

Ten years later that man is running a multimillion-dollar business he started from scratch while unemployed.

Example 2

A few years after her divorce, a woman is living a wearisome life in quiet despair. Her youthful hopes of marrying the man of her dreams and building a life together have not worked out.

As a single mother, she's had her emotional reserves drained away by the demands of raising her children alone and taking care of all the bills and responsibilities. Fatigue is constant, and the grinding disappointment of how things have turned-out weighs her down.

After an uneventful evening her daughter asks if she can have a new dress for an upcoming school dance. As the mother begins to explain in a resigned voice why her old dress will have to do, suddenly—inexplicably—this simple conversation triggers something deep within her and she becomes defiantly indignant.

Suddenly—inexplicably—fueled by a mother's love and a woman's grit, there arises, for lack of a better word, a fury within her. And it's the direct opposite of the feelings of help-lessness that had filled her soul to the brim just two minutes before this incidental conversation.

The change inside her is as complete as when one awak-ens from sleep. She sets her mind like a flint toward one unchangeable decision: "I will not live like this another day! My children are going to have a happy life full of good things.

And I will make it happen starting tomorrow by every means available, even if I have to do every step of it alone!"

She gets busy. She makes inquiries. She starts to *act*. In fact, she cannot help but act—and act immediately. She is compelled to. She is *obsessed*. Her one intention, one single point of focus, now commands every resource of her being.

She has accounting skills, and someone she knows at church helps her get a better job with a start-up firm as an assistant to the firm's chief accountant. Intent on making the most of her new position, she learns all she can about the business when not occupied with her duties inside the accounting department.

Three years later, there are personnel changes, and she is promoted to head accountant. Two more years pass, and the company starts to have financial troubles. When the firm's executive board is less than satisfied with the company president's explanations, the head accountant—*this woman*—is sent for. And she *can* explain to them what is happening to the small firm's profits, and why.

At the end of the meeting, she is called back into the room. To her absolute shock, *she* is the new company president!

Three more years pass, and a larger firm acquires the start-up. As the now indispensable head of the growing company—*a company in an industry she did not even know existed when her obsession was birthed eight years earlier*—she learns that, instead of losing her job with the new owners, the one stipulation of the purchase is that she agree to stay as part of the deal, and a generous increase in her already significant compensation is included.

Keep Turning Your Thoughts to Possible Solutions

Variations of these examples—literally millions of them—occur all over the world every year, proving again and again the mysterious power of an *obsession* to change a life, including yours and mine.

We have the power to change our lives, but we wait in vain when we look for that help from others or in a change of conditions outside of us. What we need is not a change of the conditions outside us, but a change inside us. Finding a solution to our need must become a fire in our bellies!

And if life has not put that fire there for us—and it is probably better if it does not have to come that way—then you and I will have to put it there for ourselves.

A specific desire that has become an emotional *need*, a gnawing need that preoccupies our mind, is the only way I know of to activate the powerful creative forces within us. That state of mind has produced every significant advancement in human history. And the only way I know of to voluntarily create that state of mind is to keep turning our thoughts to that thing or condition until a *need* for it fills our soul.

> "Since new developments are the products of a creative mind, we must therefore stimulate and encourage that type of mind in every way possible."
> —George Washington Carver

Once any idea becomes an internal need, one that dominates our thoughts, the creative force of our brain awakens and acts as a sending and receiving station. Just as a police dispatcher sends out a "be on the lookout" alert, our brain begins to filter every thought and event, sifting it for anything that will close the gap between us and that one thing. Action by the most practical means available becomes the constant assignment of our conscious and subconscious goal-seeking mental forces. Once this state of mind is reached the goal-seeking is happening even when we are unaware of it. Once in this condition, circumstances matter nothing at all. Whatever you call it, once the soul of a man or woman is attuned to the frequency of that goal and intensely seeking it, a way to it or its equivalent good will be found or created. When this occurs, we have literally *unchained our brain*. Our brain then becomes a living, goal-seeking, creative machine that seeks the path to its assigned target 24/7.

Any idea we focus upon until our minds will not leave it alone will, in varying lengths of time, lead to inspired thoughts, opportunities recognized, and action by the most practical means available in our normal daily life. And unless some extreme circumstance produces it involuntarily, the only way to create that state of mind is to do it ourselves, no matter how long it takes.

That condition has become my habitual state regarding the writing of these books, and soon, I must repeat the process to the purpose of getting them to you. I will not die having contributed to no one's life but my own!

Here are a few self-directed, voluntary obsessions that changed history:

- Perplexed by the high mortality rate because of infections after surgery, a series of scientists labored for years over a microscope to confirm the direct link between lack of sanitation and infectious microbes. This resulted in experimentation leading to the first procedures for sterilization during surgery, published by Joseph Lister in 1867.

- Another scientist, driven by the same focus of thought, worked for seven years to find a vaccine to stop the plague of polio. After creating the first successful vaccine, the gifted and unassuming American research scientist Jonas Salk literally gave the formula to the world for free and changed human history.

- After the boll weevil destroyed the cotton-based economy of the southeast United States, a quiet and humble African American scientist did something simple and remarkably intelligent to solve the regions problem. He planted the seed of every commercially viable crop in the red dirt of the region to see which would grow the best. He finally determined that the peanut thrived in the red clay soil and focused his attentions as a chemist and botanist upon discovering the wealth of commercial uses hidden in the simple peanut.

- George Washington Carver's discoveries resurrected the region's economy. In fact, Carver's concentrated thought upon something as obscure as a peanut brought such prosperity to the south that a statue celebrating the boll weevil was erected in Enterprise, Coffee County, Alabama, and remains to this day.

Don't tell me you cannot do the same type of thing by using self-directed thought for yourself. If you desire it intensely enough, God can turn a peanut-sized thought of your own into a new life for you. Men and women who were following their own desires built every business, founded every house of worship, and created every convenience you will use this very day. Successful men and women focus their thoughts. The rest of humanity lets their minds idle away on the mundane instead of harnessing their thoughts to proactively create a more desirable life.

I vacation often with my family in Scottsdale, Arizona. On one of our trips, I saw once again an example of the power of an obsession. We went to an Italian eatery named Oregano's, themed around 1950s Americana. The restaurant is a true delight of sensations of the sights, songs, and tastes of that era, all transporting the patron to a happy and unusually pleasant experience during the meal.

My server saw me looking around and taking everything in. Unsolicited, he told me with pride the story of the restaurant's origin:

The man who started Oregano's was a flight attendant. He was obsessed with the idea of creating a restaurant that reminded him of his childhood, but he didn't have the money. His enthusiasm and determination eventually convinced another airline employee to put up her house as collateral for a loan to finance the first restaurant. There are now thirteen, and three more are under construction.

My server then said, "This place looks like a professional restaurant designer with experience in the décor of the era did it, but they didn't. Everything you see and hear came from this one man's mind. *He is obsessed with this place!*"

The Formation of Obsession

Every man and woman who has built anything bigger than a shoebox will tell you what I am telling you: if we think about something long enough it will begin to actually live within us and take concrete form around us.

I have had that experience. As you know by now, when the idea was presented to my mind to write books, it was most unwelcome. Nevertheless, once I recognized the source of the thought, I considered it a duty and—very grudgingly—began.

I thought about the subject matter and wrote, poorly, every day for four years. I had no talent of which I was aware of for writing, and that truth was becoming more painfully obvious to me by the day. Nevertheless, I dryly persisted.

Then, after four consecutive years of consistent thought upon this one object, I began to experience a subtle change. I went from sullen about "having to write" to becoming slightly optimistic and interested.

After half a year more, my mind became preoccupied with this work; constructive thoughts and more compelling ways of expression came to my mind. Six months more, and I was rising in the middle of the night to capture an unbidden flash of thought to improve a single sentence.

> We are more than just flesh and bones. There's a certain spiritual nature and something of the mind that we can't measure. We can't find it. With all our sophisticated equipment, we cannot monitor or define it, and yet it's there.
> —Ben Carson, Neurosurgeon

Awake or asleep, I could not stop the creative flow, *and I no longer had to make myself think about it.* I was being carried along in a current I myself had created.

Eventually, I became constantly preoccupied with the most compelling way to capture and express every thought. You are now reading the product of an obsession that started as a grudging duty. How much shorter would the five-year time frame have been had it begun with interest and desire?

Honestly, my own example is as much practical instruction as any man or woman needs that is sincere about improving their life. Within a year or two you could be consumed with a specific desire that has the power to create its own fulfillment no matter where your life is now.

To voluntarily cultivate this state of mind we have but to focus upon a desired object, purpose, or set of conditions until our thoughts continuously turn to it without any conscious effort on our part then, continue until it becomes an emotional need.

How long that takes is not predictable, but it must be done. Our life will not be changed by thoughts that are nothing more than dissatisfactions, wishes, and wants.

According to Orison Swett Marden—the 19th-century inspirational author whose words changed my life—Thomas Edison responded to a question about how he created so many inventions with this statement: "You do something all day long, don't you? Everyone does. The only trouble is that they do it about a great many things and I do it about one."

To cultivate an obsession to write compelling books—an obsession that admittedly, I created without realizing what I was doing at the time—took five years of consistently holding the idea in my mind and working on it a little every day. After that, without realizing it, I would just be going through the normal activities of my day while the thoughts you are now reading would surface without any conscious intention.

> *A powerful mind is not the result of intellect but of simplicity, clarity, and focus*

In the beginning my thoughts had little to no influence upon me, until they became habitual. At that point, years of near-fruitless frustration were replaced by the actual creation of the desired object *flowing out from within me.* Even though in my case it took years, if I had spent those years to no specific mental purpose, I would have been the same number of years older but with nothing potentially life-changing taking shape.

By the way, it's important to remember that although, as in my case, years may be required, the time it takes to give vague desires focus and emotional power is itself well-used time.

I am unable to pursue two thoughts at once. Some can, maybe you can, but I do not do well when I divide my focus. So, perhaps, as in my case, you need to keep at it until you can clarify your life's next definite major purpose down to one thing. A powerful mind is not the result of intellect but of simplicity, clarity, sustained focus, and intention.

And once you have created the emotional state of *needing* what you want, the switch from thinking about it to seeking it will be automatic. Just as a magnet attracts iron particles—there is an observable force of the universe by which like things are attracted to like things—everything required for the realization of your desire will begin to move toward you by the indefinable but observable "magnetic" force of your mental frequency calling for it. Our brains truly are sending and receiving stations that span the planet, or perhaps the Universe for all I know.

Strictly speaking, we do not attract what we think about. You and I attract what we *are*. We think about something to bring it to life inside us. We want our soul to vibrate to that frequency.

Here is the mental process of creation put as simply as possible:

I wish … I want … I *need* … I Got.

I Wish … I Want … *I Need* … I GOT!

Aware of it or not, intelligently used or not, we each direct our own life to a purpose or drift along. You must want what you say you want and want it strongly enough to keep thinking about it and keep thinking about it with the intention of getting it! Talk to yourself about it, ponder it, and take steps toward it as ideas come to you or opportunity affords. Eventually the objective takes on its own life within you and starts to pull each of you toward the other.

Your part is to create the need, not the "how." That will be provided by the Universal Law that like things attract like things. When the *Why* is strong, the *How* will come.

The dilemma so many of us wrestle with is that we want something that is beyond our power to arrange or possess right now, but don't know what to do about it. But the "how" or the "way" is rarely known by anyone when they decide to do something new. That is not how successful people succeed. Your job is to decide what one thing you want *next* above all others and then decide that you *will* have it. If you must see a way before you commit, you will cut yourself off from a great many blessings in this life that had your name on them.

The state of mind known as obsession will produce whatever is needed to go from "here" to "there" when the "there" has been clearly defined and has become a *need*.

The kingdom you are drawing from is within you. It is not logical or sequential. It is not connected to or dependent upon such things. It places no time limits and makes no judgements based on your history or current conditions. It is a living and effervescent well of life that flows out from us and can, in one step, move us somewhere that would normally require five years of labor. Christ described the nature of this spiritual Life-Force in the gospel of John 7:38, "Out of his belly shall flow rivers of living waters."

This Life-Force (which is within you and me right now, though it may be dormant) is creative. It is our Makers likeness, awaiting our decision to partake in His work of intentional creation and increase. Indeed, we were put here for that purpose. The expression of life everywhere, plant or animal, seeks fulfillment and growth.

Am I a mystic? No! I only know that for the wide-awake man or woman an observable power exists that responds to intense desire and intention. Though it does seem mystical, this is in fact observable universal law that acts very much like and is as predictable as gravity.

When a man or woman has a goal that is clear and specific, and desired intensely, then he or she will activate, or perhaps become, a magnetic force that changes what moves into and away from his or her life. No preexisting conditions or materials are needed. All will be supplied on the existing life-path.

When we must have a thing—*because the thing has us*—a way will be made to it or to its most beneficial equivalent.

As a boy, I saw what happens when a man fails to fulfill his commitments. At about ten years of age, I made up my mind that I would never abandon my family and they would never live in want. Years later, now a young man, I was driving a police car for a living and had no idea what to do to bring about my definite major purpose of comfortable circumstances for my family, but I would not let the thought go. I couldn't without betraying myself, but doing *what?* I had no other skills!

I knew nothing of the principles I am writing about now. I just knew that for me, I *had to* provide a better life for my future wife and children than my job and skills could provide. But the question was always how? Doing what? I had no education beyond high school, no money, no connections, no other experience, and no training other than police work. No matter how I searched my mind, I could see no answer, no options, no ideas … *no way!*

After many years of stewing in this definite desire, the opportunity to go to work for my stepfather was presented. However, in no way did I think that was my answer, nor did I suspect it for the many years afterward while I toiled. I did not like the roofing business, which was his line of work. I went into the business because it was at least a step toward my goal of getting away from living payday to payday. I stayed with it while I hoped and prayed for a better opportunity.

Time proved that the opportunity I was seeking was already there. I had "stepped into the flow" where at least there was a current flowing in the general direction I wished to go. Thomas Edison is credited with the observation, "Opportunity is missed by most people because it is dressed in overalls and looks like work." That happened to me.

Over time, the business provided something closely approximating the life I had dreamed of. Why? Because the creative force within me was influencing the events of my life to conform them to my one desire. You and I do not need to understand this process any better than that. I do not know how a watch works, but I can still use one to give me the correct time. And that is all I need to know about a watch to use it!

When you are seeking a better life, it is not necessary that any single opportunity has the path to all you desire. If it offers more than is possible to you on the path you are on now, and you are not opposed to doing it, step in the direction that is going up. That is all I did, as I was only presented with one opportunity.

The Power to Change Conditions is Already Yours

Our part in the creative process is to decide purposefully (and perhaps prayerfully) what our next change in conditions or material objective is. When due to sustained thought, which may take time, you find your mind turning constantly toward that intention but without considering all the obstacles, the creative process has begun in the very real but unseen realm of mental and emotional energy. Our creative faculty does the work of arranging compatible people, events, coincidences, connections, happenstances and flashes of thought, without our conscious awareness of when or how.

Strategic Coach founder Dan Sullivan's observed, that after years of coaching successful men and women, that their plans were not achieved by learning the *how*, but by deciding what they were going to do, then becoming connected to the persons or events to get it done, which he calls the right "Who's." That principle was discussed earlier in this work. The Bible reinforces this in the gospel of Luke 6:38. "Give and it shall be given unto you; good measure, pressed down, and shaken together, and running over, shall men (and women, of course) give into your bosom." When we *give* our mind a specific task, answers and needs are *given* when our thoughts hold to the task with strong desire.

God answers prayers by arranging encounters with the right events or people. Trust the creative process to know how to arrange what you require by the most practical means available along your life path. If a particular line of thought can't get traction with you, find another way to think about it. Do not dwell on the current limiting conditions and practicalities.

This Force, or Spirit, or spark of the Divine within, whatever it is, will reveal the way in steps. Even though you cannot see a way, if it is important to you, clarify and hold your vision.

All that exists came from exactly this process: your car from Mr. Ford's mind, the conditioned air in your office from the mind of Mr. Carrier, and your plane ticket from the Wright brothers. Big and small, visible and not yet created, our lives are supplied by someone who decided upon and sustained a specific line of thought.

During the writing of my books, I have not contemplated the selling of them, but the desire to complete the writing is unceasing. And until they are written, *that is the only desire I need.*

Frankly, when I think about selling non-fiction self-help books to a digital-age, five-second sound-bite generation, the long odds against success can sometimes be discouraging, so I do not dwell on it. When it is time, getting the work into your hands will become my sole focus. Then, I will confront the task and rely on God's ingenuity to supply whatever I lack to reveal the way.

Keeping Your Focus

This process sometimes happens involuntarily due to circumstances, as in my young life when a desire to provide financial well-being for my future family unconsciously became a need, but if it has not happened involuntarily for you, you can create something approximating those emotional conditions by many methods. Here are a few:

- looking at photographs of your goal
- listening to audio recordings and/or uplifting sermons/ lectures
- reviewing or writing out your desire daily (my method)

- reading encouraging books such as this one regularly (essential to me)
- Speaking faith-building "I can do this" conversations aloud to yourself

At various times I use them all. And it might be worth noting again that I created an emotional need to complete my writings simply by thinking about it and working on it every day for five years, though most of those years the effort felt very dry. Sustained actions, even though small at the start, evidently have a cumulative effect.

Do whatever helps you to keep your mind occupied with your definite purpose until the desire gains a life of its own.

Once the line of thought becomes involuntary, it will become stronger on its own. In the writing of this book, that transformation took four-and-a-half years. When I began, I had to make myself write and it was dry, toilsome labor to me. Now, I would complete the books if I had to write them on a prison wall!

I have become obsessed with the information that the five *Common Sense for a Prosperous Life* books offer the readers. I want to write it. I *need* to write it. I *must* write it. I reach for my computer and let my fingers touch the keypad as my eyes search the words on the screen again and again to improve them.

I am emotionally attached to it, as one would be to a living thing. I am no longer writing so much as the thoughts are flowing out of me. If I were to stop, it would be like "fire shut up in my bones." (Jeremiah 20:9, NKJV)

All this life-changing power came from a single impulse of thought that was stayed upon until it possessed me; an idea that I felt was improbable to the point of absurdity when I began.

I am nearing the end of the writing portion of this life-changing assignment. I will soon need to change my focus from writing to selling, another statistical improbability of huge proportions. I do not yet know the first step of the "how" for that. But I do know that the *How* will come because the *Why* is strong. Much of the *How* will probably be supplied by encouraging small events, inspired thoughts, and timely introductions to key people unknown to me now.

As I type these very words, I am an unknown person writing a series of books intended to be a reference manual for the most important issues of life—money, business, marriage, and private temptations and choices that can derail our plans. My Common Sense for a Prosperous Life book series is written to spark a healthy ambition in men and women to make more of themselves in character and in capital and be lovingly wise role models for their children. And I am doing this even though I have no public fame nor any knowledge of the book business at all; a business in which fewer than one in many tens of thousands will ever succeed.

> You don't always need a plan. Sometimes you just need to breathe, trust, let go, and see what happens.
> —Mandy Hale

Despite the odds, it is my responsibility and yours to use our life to do that which we feel is our purpose as each season of our life unfolds. According to Bronnie Ware, an end-of-life care worker who wrote *The Top Five Regrets of the Dying,* the most common and most painful regret at the end of life is looking back on the thing that we feel we should have done during our time here, but never had the courage to do.

You and I still have time to avoid this, the single most painful human regret at the end of life. And my writings will teach you how to avoid other common regrets too. My books could just as well have been titled "How to Get to the End of Your Life Without Major Regrets," for avoiding our common pitfalls and using our gifts despite our imperfections are the entire subject matter.

When everything inside a man or woman *must have it* this creative process which defies our reasoning mind will create a way to it or to its equivalent good. It even overcomes our faults, which all have. This force is variously referred to as universal law, the law of attraction, mental vibration, or spiritual energy. Whatever it is, I consider it our "genetic marker" from God whose creative spark is within us. This creative force is activated by a strong emotional need. Like my watch, I don't need to understand how it works to use it.

In other words, I am not writing about some esoteric secret spiritual knowledge. No, I am talking about the eminently practical way in which we are made—when we focus on something our life moves toward it. To begin to use this power correctly quit focusing on your frustration and start focusing on the solution to it. The reason most people never harness this power is that their intention is too fleeting for its effects to take hold; they stare at the problem and glance at solutions. Reverse that and you're on your way up.

I am calling your attention to something that is very real, but observable only by effect. I can't see the wind, but I know it exists because I can see and feel its influence on the things around me. That is all that is going on here. This force that we cannot see, I can categorically state exists because I can see its effects across all human history. This critical subject so vital to our preparation for life is totally neglected in our academic instruction.

I am attempting to explain something so predictable that I invite you to present these thoughts for review to anyone you know who has built something of note. I believe that without a single exception they will tell you, "I was not thinking in these terms at the time, but in hindsight, that is exactly what happened."

How much proof do we need before we will begin to use this powerful faculty for our own benefit? Proofs stand in material form all around us. Every living thing God created from plant to human has an inborn desire for an upward reach. Look at how every leaf around you reaches for more height and sunlight. Look and consider that the hearts of every responsible man and woman wants more for themselves and their children.

We don't seek this upward desire; the desire is innate. Is it not logical that the Creator would also have given humankind a way to facilitate that God-given, healthy desire for more life?

This thing that I am describing—whatever label you give it—is it!

Keeping Progress Simple

In *The Entry-Level CEO*, the third in my Common Sense for a Prosperous Life book series, you will find useful information about how to make a big goal and long odds feel "do-able." I will not repeat it here, but the book is worth buying just to have those thoughts at the ready for your own benefit. Because, again, a clear *what* with a passionate *why* will lead you to the *how*—even though early on it is step by faltering step.

So if the thought of selling a million books defeats my spirit when I am finished writing and the time comes to sell, then I will set a goal to sell a thousand books—or one hundred. I will find some goal that will keep me moving in the right direction without overwhelming me mentally or emotionally.

Whatever you focus on, you get more of. The small-steps approach is a simple thing I do to keep myself moving. If I can believe to sell one hundred books, and I can, then when that is done maybe I can believe to sell one hundred more. But if instead I think of the fact that only one in tens of thousands of authors sell enough books to justify the time spent writing them, I will be defeated before I even start.

> *Whatever you focus on, you get more of, so focus of solutions.*

What we give our attention to we give our life-energy to. Emotional energy is the locus of our will to do. By using a goal, even a modest one, that produces a feeling of "I can do that" our will to act grows. And the reverse is true. If we think too long-term, we will decrease our will to move forward. When you tackle a large goal and feel overwhelmed, you need to shrink the task. You can make everything a problem if you think too far ahead.

When we see men and women of accomplishment, we all marvel, but what do you think goes on in their minds that produces these outcomes? They are thinking about doing something specific constantly, and they believe they can do it. Common sense, right? You and I can certainly do more of that.

Most of us tend to mentally dwell on the things in our life that we don't like. That has been my most glaring fault for too much of my life. Achievers are usually focused on progress and only mildly aware of dissatisfactions. Out of necessity, I have developed a helpful way to use my reflexively critical thoughts to move me forward. When I realize that my thoughts have become self-critical or focused too much on my dissatisfactions, I ask myself a question: "Considering all these concerns of mine, what is *the one thing* that would have the greatest positive effect if I were to change it right now?" Then, I make doing that my one immediate goal.

You can use self-critical thoughts, which most of us have from time to time, to find needed changes that *you are in full control of right now*. After each improvement has become your relative norm repeat the process. Amazingly, just two or three of these actions will greatly improve your opinion of yourself and lift your optimism and confidence, sometimes within just a few months!

The will to reach for a more abundant and fulfilling life comes from an improving opinion of our own self and taking steps that feel "do-able."

When I was nineteen a man took the time to inspire me with an ambition to do something worthwhile with my life.

He changed my life and the life of my future wife and family. Before my time here ends, I want to do that for many others.

I am still repairing homes for my living, but I am willing to look past that and write these thoughts and get them into the marketplace. That must be done no matter what happens afterward, and I *can* do *that* much now. As you read my words in some future year let it be proof enough for you that you *can* take charge of your own life.

Am I saying we can control everything that happens, everything that comes into our lives? If you mean in absolute terms, no. I have heard that claim made but I do not believe it. Ultimate control is the prerogative of the Creator alone. But ask me, "Can we set a different course and get to a different place, no matter our current circumstances?" and to that question I say, "Absolutely."

This one truth controls all creative human activity: **When the *why* is strong, the *how* will come.**

I wanted, and won, a better life than I was going to get by continuing to take whatever life handed me at birth. After my military service in law enforcement, civilian police work was comfortable and convenient to me, but I had to take my one opportunity to get to higher levels of income when presented or stay in that line of work for life. Then, decades later, to my surprise, I was led to write books that would, in practical terms, help others to make more of their own lives as well. We must all take our shot and begin to climb out for ourselves before we can help anyone else.

The destination is certainly important to us, we need it for our motivation. But the journey to get what we want is where the shaping and the strengthening occur, and these things are not possible if we choose an uncontested life. The healthy ambition for *more* of all the good things in life motivates us and this ambition serves as His workshop for our souls. In the end, the shiny things that motivated us fade a little. Use and years temper the luster of all new things. But a man or woman nearing full stature, self-approving and independent, confident and cheerful, calm and encouraging, living in gratitude and helping others—that comes from the struggle and remains with us forever. It shines brighter with the years.

In the end, who we have become is the only thing we take with us: Did we do what we should have done with our life while we were here? Did we become someone that properly uses the gifts they were given? Did we openly express and demonstrate love of self and others? Did we serve and affirm our family? Our friends? Our faith? Did we confront our private hindrances, clean up our own life, and use our time to a good purpose?

And what causes our life to end without the joy of these things that are far more excellent than leisure and pleasure? Irresolute drifting … seeking only the safe and familiar … the desire to see the way before we begin … letting the odds determine our future … avoiding uncertainty and continuing the habits we ourselves disapprove of. All these my books confront in practical terms.

This contested life is not for everyone. For some reason, it was for me, though each bit of progress came slowly and with much internal resistance. Though there are many authors of much greater wealth and accomplishment, I was "called" to write to the common man and woman and show them in simple terms the common sense that will give them an uncommon life. This is my purpose. Christ said that it was not the well but the sick that needed a physician; and it is not the gifted but the common, the struggling, the uncertain and doubtful that I bring my message of hope and common-sense instruction to.

Considering what we have discussed, is it possible that the disappointments of your life have prepared you to offer the marketplace something that can enrich the life of others and reward you? If nothing comes to mind, keep doing what you are doing and ask God to show you at the right time.

Because of my truly kind but very irresponsible father I had a lifelong sensitivity to men who are a poor example for their children. As a result, I became committed to responsibility and family. To my surprise, I was eventually led to encourage others to this purpose through my writings.

I grew up in a home with a struggling but cheerful single mother of three who had no support. Today, I am writing books that will inspire men to be the fathers and husbands and lifelong-partners they should be.

I grew up in a home where money was scarce. My books will show every reader how using a little common sense when making decisions can make their lives more stable, prosperous and happy.

I grew up hungry to escape the paycheck-to-paycheck life, but with no idea how. I struggled for decades in blue-collar lines of work. But in those struggles I learned insights that will cut the journey to financial independence in half for many and inspire many others to step out on opportunity or make their own.

The years when God was distant and the road hard were not pleasant to go through, but my obsession not to repeat the failings I had seen—not my skills or gifts or intellect, for they were too few—eventually turned it all into grist for the mill. Very often, the light we bring to the world is born from our own dark seasons. The brilliance of gold is only revealed after going through the fire.

I know from personal experience that during the difficult times one can see nothing good coming from the trials, but if we will not surrender our hope and somehow keep "the fire in our belly" alive for something better, the Great Alchemist, the Way-Maker, the Promise-Keeper will *make all things work together for our good.* (Romans 8:28, NKJV)

The problems we so resent and see as unfair treatment, or even as a violation of our trust by an uncaring God, have future benefits far greater than can be imagined when we are in them. I think for most of us there are times when God kicks all the crutches out and steps back to see if we will trust Him without any support. Emotional survival in those times is difficult for sure, but there are two unchanging truths: first, where there is life there is hope, and second, no matter what the situation is, *God is aware, and God always works the night shift!*

Most of us will give in to despair for a short season every now and then. But there comes a time when just like Rocky Balboa in the Rocky movie, you just refuse to give up. I tell you this from experience: There will come a time, if you stand and glare at life and dare it to do its damnedest, life itself will say, "Doesn't he know when he's beat? Just give the damn fool what he wants!" The men and women that keep going through the dark times will drink today's tears from champagne flutes tomorrow.

Our Thoughts Become Our Life

Consider the thoughts I am sharing with you in relation to any success story of which you are aware. Consider them in relation to the very words you are reading now, though at this moment, I am an unknown blue-collar contractor that can't name fifty people who will buy even one of my five books.

Consider this information in relation to the inspired thought that at some point may be presented to your own mind. An emotional need makes the way when there seems to be no way **because the mental obsession *is* the way**.

Do you desire better housing for your family? The desire for an adequate and pleasant home is God-given and approved of by Him. Do you desire reliable, debt-free transportation? That too, is God-approved. Do you desire to be the one sharing aid with others instead of needing it? God-approved, again. Do you desire to see your life count for more than a struggle for daily existence? God-Approved!

It is said, "Thoughts are things." And they are, because every material thing, whether created by God or humankind, began as nothing more than a thought in someone's mind. But instead of being dismissed, the idea had life breathed into it by a brain that, intentionally or otherwise, incubated it until it had a life of its own inside that man or woman's spirit. This is what the Bible describes as good seed falling on good ground. (Mathew 13:23)

The evidence is all around you. High intellect is not needed. Almost all the skills we so admire in others were acquired *after* they made their decision.

The wise will begin to participate. The ones who complain that they can't catch a break or get the help they need will keep letting their life slip away.

A life filled with failure, lack, complaints, feelings of exhaustion and discouragement, and unchallenged moral weaknesses is the result of an unfocused, undisciplined, irresolute mind. So choose and develop a passionate purpose!

Just as fire converts everything in its path to fuel, a strong emotional desire that becomes a *need* will filter whatever crosses your lifepath and weigh its usefulness to the one purpose. It will begin to attract helpful forces, events, and people into your life. In time it *must* have an effect!

Talent is overrated. Skills are acquired. A life of increase has only two requirements: a clearly defined intention and a desire strong enough to push through discouragements. I have addressed both in this book.

Protect Your Progress

Without personal character, success is nearly impossible to attain or keep, if attained. And until there is an emotionally compelling reason, few will have a will strong enough to confront their moral weaknesses and awaken their creative powers. I think you should consider including in your goals one character improvement a year. Most men and women have no more than two or three bad habits that will hold them back. If we eliminated just one weakness a year, within five years most of us would be so transformed in self-confidence that staying where we are financially would not even be possible.

However, I think it is worth mentioning that while we are improving, we must guard against becoming overly critical of our self. In matters of eliminating personal weaknesses, it is the direction that you are deliberately moving in rather than the nearness to perfection that you should celebrate. Self-reproach helps no one. Acknowledging our victories and the decreasing the occasions for disappointment will allow us to continue to improve without becoming so discouraged that we give up. "I am better at this than I used to be" is a powerful tonic for change. (My fifth book in the series *Private Choices, Public Power* discusses this subject in detail.)

Natural Laws Reflect Spiritual Realities

We live in a universe of such divine order that the position of stars can be known with equal precision ten seconds or ten thousand years from now. In some inscrutable way in this precise and exacting universe, a strong desire for a specific thing will connect you to incidences consistent with that desire *and begin to move the things needful for its creation toward you.*

The great explorer and mountaineer W. H. Murray, whose life story is too remarkable to recap here, wrote, "Concerning all acts of initiative (and creation), there is one elemental truth, the ignorance of which kills countless ideas and splendid plans: that the moment one commits oneself, then providence moves too. A whole stream of events issues from the decision, raising in one's favor all manner of unforeseen incidents, meetings, and material assistance, which no man could have dreamt would have come his way."

During a family conversation in which this truth was being shared with our daughters, my wife explained it to our girls this way:

There is a spiritual force within us that is like a river. It flows out of us and its influence removes or attracts the common things in our life around us. When we truly decide to do something, we think about it almost continuously. When that happens, ways to do that thing begin to come to us. Helpful events begin to appear, often in ways that we could never have thought of. This is our spirit at work and is part of God which He placed within us.

This universe is more than a meaningless combination of physical matter. It is a place where both natural and spiritual forces interact and cause movement, because the Spirit of its Creator, our Creator, fill it. No matter what your circumstances are now, there is a way higher. Redirect your emotional energy from discouragement or resigned acceptance to one of single-minded, emotional intention. Get angry, determined, or passionate, whatever works for you. Pick a target, look up, talk up, and start moving up. Keep talking and looking around and stay down.

Yes, this universe is more than its physical properties or the sciences that seek to interpret it. It is filled with an energy which in some mysterious but observable way responds to our dominating thoughts. Don't you doubt it for one minute.

This is not mysticism or philosophy. It is provable as it can be plainly observed in human affairs. Gravity is invisible, but it affects the movement of the universe because there are laws that determine why things move. Those laws govern planets and people with equal precision because *like things always attract like things.*

The comforts we wish to enjoy, the good that we wish to accomplish, the man or woman we wish to become, are all waiting on our decision to reach for them with clear intention and cultivated, increased desire. And we become better men and women by taking that upward journey. Practical ideas and events result from sustained desires along a single and straight line of thought.

If you must fight for a thought to be of interest to you, choose another that will move you in the same direction but sits more easily on your mind. For example, I have a goal to be financially independent of my home improvement business. I will probably still choose to do it, but I don't want to need it. I must acquire more rental homes to do that. If I consider everything that will be required, the thoughts don't work for me. So instead, I think about adding two more rental homes. It's the same plan and the same direction, but it is an easier thought to hold, and it's the next step anyway. If a desire can't get mental traction, it does not mean the direction is wrong, only that you may need to choose a closer step on the path.

When applying this, we don't need to decide what we should do with the rest of our lives; we often simply don't know the answer to that. But we can all identify some one thing that is worth our focus until we have it. Whatever that is for you, here is something that I can assure you of: If you think about it long enough your feelings will gradually morph from, "How could I *ever* get there?" to, "This is not as improbable as I thought. There are ways this could be done."

In my own case, the first step to being a successful author is to write something worth reading. The dozens of other improbable things necessary to get my books to you don't need to be considered yet. I will get to my desired destination by keeping each goal within reach of sixty minutes of well-used time each day.

What would happen if we asked ourselves, "What do I really want next that would mean the most to me, that would make the biggest difference in enjoying my life?"—and then gave sixty minutes a day to it? Settling that question, and then dwelling on it until there is an emotional need to have it, will unchain your magnificently powerful creative brain.

And now reader, will you awaken your dormant powers? Will you begin to require more of yourself than meaningless entertainments and aimless thoughts? Will you stop letting the "facts" of your life chain you to a treadmill? Will you quit waiting for someone else to give you what you think you lack? Will you wake up the powers within your own soul? *Will you come to your own aid?*

The legendary genie of Aladdin's lamp responded to wishes, but there is a very real genie inside you. That genie will respond to any desire that has been nurtured until you *need* it.

Unchain Your Brain from the frail human reasoning that quotes the odds and recites the "facts." The fact-sifting portion of your brain is of great daily service, but it is neither powerful nor creative. It assists with rational choices to avoid danger and meet immediate needs. But it leaves the powers of your soul, and universal laws, and faith and God, out of every calculation it makes. Limiting your life to what you can see a way to do is the modern-day equivalent of eating from the Tree of Knowledge instead of the Tree of Life.

When we make a decision that sweeps every reservation aside, our brain is so designed that it will immediately leap into action. In that instant we begin a new life, though it may take years to produce the harvest. I am betting on it by writing these words for you to read in future years. Will you join me on this road less traveled by taking your own upward journey? I pray you will. And it is my hope that in some future year, you and I will scarcely believe who we have become.

***Did I not say to you that if you would
believe you would see the glory of God?***
(The words of Jesus Christ. John 11:40, NKJV)

ABOUT THE AUTHOR

Mark Ashe is the owner of a successful home improvement business in Atlanta. He and his wife of over thirty years have three grown daughters. They enjoy life on their 40-acre farm in the rolling hills of north Georgia, traveling with friends or with their daughters, and great meals shared with close friends. Mark went from being a policeman to debt free and financially independent by his mid-forty's.

Mark writes and speaks with compelling clarity on "common sense for the uncommon life." A wealthy financial adviser has described Mark's writings as "a PhD level course in successful living."

Mark's premise, and the proof of his life, is that an average man or woman can attain surprising success when the desire to do so is strong and the major decisions of life are made with a practical sensibility that his books bring to life through personal examples.

Connect at www.markashe.com